Doing Qualitative Research Using QSR NUD*IST

Doing Qualitative Research Using QSR NUD*IST

Celia Gahan and Mike Hannibal

SAGE Publications
London • Thousand Oaks • New Delhi

First published 1998. Reprinted 1999 (twice)

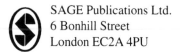 SAGE Publications Ltd.
6 Bonhill Street
London EC2A 4PU

SAGE Publications Inc.
2455 Teller Road
Thousand Oaks, California 91320

SAGE Publications India Pvt. Ltd.
32, M–Block Market
Greater Kailash I
New Delhi 110 048

British Library Cataloguing in Publication data

A catalogue record for this book is
available from the British Library

ISBN 0–7619–5390–6 (pbk)

Library of Congress catalog record available

Typeset by Mentor Consulting Pty Ltd, Australia
Printed in Great Britain by Cromwell Press, Trowbridge, Wiltshire

CONTENTS

Acknowledgements

Throughout the development of this book and the workshops that have contributed to it, a number of people have supported and encouraged us. Significant amongst them are: Lyn Richards who has been unflagging in her efforts to offer review and make positive suggestions when the going got really tough; Simon Ross, our editor, for his unyielding commitment; David Russell for his friendship and mentorship throughout the years; Nadarajah Sriskandarajah for his continuing belief in us; Helen ten Dam and Graham Beaumont for their loyalty and support; and all those researchers who have come to our workshops and have participated with enthusiasm and energy over the last eight years—without all of you the book would not have happened.

Celia & Mike
Melbourne, 1998

PREFACE

This book was written to provide a resource to researchers from a range of methodological traditions to assist them in exploring and understanding how QSR NUD•IST may be utilised in qualitative research processes. It is not intended as a text book on methodology nor is it a computer manual. Rather it is an easy to read and use resource, which covers enough of the technical stuff to enable researchers to utilise—and enjoy using—QSR NUD•IST in their research.

The book draws heavily on our experience over the last eight years of using the software in research projects and conducting training in the use of QSR NUD•IST. We have tried to make it practical but relevant to the diversity of researchers who everyday work with qualitative material. For this reason it does not adopt a particular approach to research but rather focuses on understanding qualitative research tasks and matching these to the tools provided in QSR NUD•IST.

We see QSR NUD•IST as a *tool kit* to assist researchers. Like any other tool it needs time spent on getting to know it, using it and thinking about how it fits with "what I'm trying to achieve".

The book can not, nor is it intended to replace the *User's Manual*, but rather it complements the resources which are provided with the software.

In the book we have adopted a project focus and work through the stages of "doing" a project using QSR NUD•IST Version 4. Throughout the book we will refer to the software as N4. Some areas of the software we have not covered in any detail, especially how N4 links with other specialized programs. A wide range of other resources including comprehensive bibliographies and technical support, are available to you through N4's on–line Help system, the QSR email forum and World Wide Web resources.

We are using N4 on a Macintosh and all the reproduced screen displays are from this platform. There are a number of differences between the Macintosh and PC platforms, both visually and in mouse movements. However, when operating in the software itself there are very few differences, and where these exists, they will be indicated in the text.

If you are still using QSR NUD•IST Version 3, you will find that the description of N4's tool kit generally fits, since the programs share a common architecture. While there are differences between the versions the conceptual overview of doing qualitative research using QSR NUD•IST is very relevant to both versions. There are however new ways of handling data in N4 which are not available in Version 3.

We hope that the book provides a resource which facilitates your learning in doing qualitative research using QSR NUD•IST's comprehensive tool kit—and that the journey is a valuable and enjoyable one.

1

INTRODUCING QSR
NUD•IST VERSION 4

N4 is a tool kit to assist and support individuals and groups who are engaged in qualitative research processes. As a tool kit, it does not displace you as the researcher or your processes as the central area of activity. But rather, N4 supports the processes or activities that *you* engage in as you go about the business of doing qualitative research.

Some researchers harbour a secret desire that a computer will somehow do away with the need to engage with the data—that the computer will distinguish the important bits and then make all the links between these bits. For another group of researchers, it is the underlying fear and anxiety that the computer will indeed take over the data and do things to it!

Using N4 in a project does not mean that you, as the researcher, can stop having ideas about, engaging with, getting to know your data, and building out of your analysis the story or stories to be told about *this project*. Nor does it mean that you will become the slave of the machine that will capture your project and take it to places you didn't intend to go.

N4 does provides tools to do things that you couldn't do or do so well without the software. The researcher is able to ask questions and seek answers to those questions that without N4, they could not or dared not ask. While N4 provides the tools to execute this "question—answer" interaction, these tasks are researcher directed and implemented.

This distinction between researcher and the researcher's tool kit is an important one.

If, as a researcher, I am unable to separate from my process or activity long enough to identify and name each element of that process, I risk becoming lost, swamped, stuck or disillusioned with the tool kit itself.

If I can become clearer about what it is that I am doing, I am better able to match the tools to the task at hand. Being able to name key processes enables me to orientate much better inside N4 and make it work harder to meet the demands of my process.

A question that we have often started our N4 training workshops with is: "When you are doing qualitative research, what key tasks, activities or processes are you involved in?" Researchers give many different answers to this question but there seems to be a cluster of activities which researchers *do* or are *interested in doing*, regardless of their methodological or ideological position.

The following points are some of the tasks or processes researchers have named as important to them and what they *do*. They are the starting points at which researchers have come to N4 training courses, and from there develop as their skills evolve.

- Seeing the story in complicated data and finding out what's going on;

- Sorting data into theme areas so that all the "stuff" about a theme is in one place and it can be viewed all together;

- Locating key words or phrases, sorting them and storing them in one place so that they can be reviewed;

- Linking ideas together;

- Comparing groups or sites or stages to see how they are different;

- Locating all answers for a question and then looking for key ideas expressed in the responses;

- Making categories for thinking about the data and to see more general shapes in the data;

- Using categories to code data and then examining each category to see what it is referring to;

- Doing the data justice—not just summarizing it but really exploring;

- Re–coding or resorting data which no longer "fits" where it was previously categorized;

- Looking to see if there are linkages between categories or theme areas;

- Testing or checking to see if a link or a pattern between categories is really there;

- Managing or knowing where all the data is, so it doesn't become lost or misplaced.

These key tasks or activities are what N4 is intended to support, to assist, and to extend—to take you to a place in your research that is much harder to reach, or even inaccessible without N4.

The next chapter presents an overview of the key tools provided in N4's kit. Each of these tools provides a way for researchers to design and direct how research tasks and activities may be implemented in N4.

As we work through N4's took kit we will be using data from a research enquiry we were involved in which explored with older people, issues of self autonomy and its expression in older life. The data includes transcriptions of 64 interviews and six group sessions, seven field note books, literature and other materials including stories written by primary school children about older people. We have called this project *Getting On*.

2

A GUIDED TOUR OF
WHAT'S INSIDE N4

This tour describes the key elements you will find inside N4, their functions and how they support and assist you to *do* qualitative research. These elements are not exhaustive of the tools available within N4, but rather are intended as a skeleton or framework which can be fleshed out and built upon.

2.1   What is a project?

Projects and what they look like are as varied as researchers and the methodological viewpoints they represent. There are however, common elements in all qualitative research projects:

- data which is messy, unstructured, usually textual and always rich;

- concepts, ideas or hunches about the data; and

- the researcher who is the creator of the concepts, ideas or hunches about the data. They design and direct how the research 'should' proceed. The researcher brings into the project 'a bag of tools' to assist them. How big this bag is, what's inside it and how well developed each tool is, varies from researcher to researcher.

A N4 project contains the same elements—data, ideas and researcher.

This tight and explicit integration of the researcher is purposeful. In N4, data is managed through the Document System, ideas are represented in the Index System, and the researcher orchestrates the ongoing interaction between data and ideas.

It is not necessary to have all the bits together before you set up a project in N4. Some projects start with only a glimmer of understanding which is expressed as a "I want to find out about..." statement. Others may be relatively well developed with significant amounts of data already collected and a well formed set of ideas or thinking about the data. Others may have the data but no clear idea about how to organise the data.

Researchers come from many different backgrounds and from a range of methodologies. This means projects have many different designs and shapes—and reflect the diversity of researchers and their methodologies. This book is not about these methodologies but rather the tool kit (N4) which supports and assists researchers to design and direct how their projects should proceed.

Whatever your beginning point, you'll gain enormous benefit from knowing the tools and making use of them early in your project.

2.2 What is the document system?

The document system offers the researcher a set of ways of managing the data which are part of a project. In N4 data is held in the document system as a document or set of documents.

N4 is able to store, search and retrieve documents or bits of documents so that you are able to work with the bits of data you want to, without having to worry about where all the other bits are, and whether or not you'll ever be able to find them again. This ability to store, sort, search and pull out parts of itself are essential to how the document system works and is its strength.

The document system is like a big bag that holds together the data documents which are part of your project. Throughout the life of your project you are able to keep placing documents into this bag and use the tools inside N4 to organise and view their contents.

N4 doesn't require that the data be typed on computer. You can handle documents in two ways—*importing* them or keeping them *external*. You can store in memos your ideas about either sort of document.

If you import a document you physically bring into N4 a copy of the actual text of the document in digital form. N4 therefore can search the *text*, as well as any *coding of the text* you may do, and it can give you back all the text that you ask to see.

Many projects have a lot of data that will never be typed onto computer. This may be books in your literature review, photographs in the drawer, handwritten letters, newspaper editorials, and so on. These can be handled in N4 as external documents.

If you don't want to import the text of a document, for example, if it is very large or not the sort of data which can be imported, you can tell N4 about it. A *reference* to the external document, and data about it, is held within the document system. N4 can't search or give you back the text, but you can still code the document, and it can tell you where to go to find the material you want.

When we started the *Getting On* project, the first data documents were transcriptions of two interviews with the first participants in the project. External documents were journal articles and book extracts, and as well, some sketches of older people drawn by local primary school children. Transcriptions of interviews were imported into N4 and the other data were managed as external documents.

2.3	**What is the index system?**	Everyday life is filled with endless detail, but we can communicate the experience, knowledge and meaning that we attribute to life and its events because we generalise. It is this abstraction or *viewing at a more general level* "things", "event" or "processes" and *how they relate to each other* which is at the heart of all the different methods of qualitative analysis.

Qualitative analysis involves the researcher thinking about data, developing ideas about it and exploring these ideas. Thinking, developing and exploring of data and ideas can occur through intuition and impression. Making analysis from those ideas requires conceptual tools to order, strengthen, enhance and bring clarity to this process. The index system is a conceptual tool to assist the researcher in this analysis process.

The index system can be seen like another big bag. In it you can put all of the categories, themes or labels that express characteristics or elements of things, events and processes, hunches and the beginnings of theories which are meaningful for this project.

In N4 each category is given a place in the index system. This place is referred to as a *node*. Each node has a numerical address, a title and definition. You may organise these nodes in various ways: as a hierarchy, as a flat structure or as unstructured or free nodes. You can store in a memo your ideas about a node.

Our earliest ideas in the *Getting On* project came from the experiences of a couple who had very recently moved into a retirement village. These ideas were about the transition from "home" to "village" and the sense of loss of autonomy and identity which appeared to be associated with the move. As we observed this couple and continued to explore with them their experience, we saw them undergo significant change in the ensuing months. Our ideas changed as we saw them rebuild identity, perceptions of self and well being as they began to participate in their new community.

The index system provides a place for you to organise and manage nodes so that what may have begun as a "formless" bag of things develops into a *system* of nodes. This system of nodes is for you to use in ongoing enquiry, searching and theory building throughout the project's life.

2.4 How does the researcher link document and index systems?

So far your project can be seen as two metaphorical bags sitting alongside each other. On one hand, you have in your big bag of documents, data which depicts life and experience of life in all its detail, complexity, richness, messiness and apparent chaos. It is the work of the index system to assist in creating abstraction, structure and pattern so that you are able to talk about the data and *tell the story* of this bag of documents.

These "bags" exist separately from each other and are different in function.

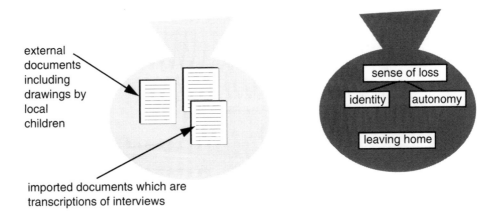

external documents including drawings by local children

imported documents which are transcriptions of interviews

The document and index systems at the early stages of the project

You can pick up just the document bag and find out what's in it. You can retrieve the text of a document and browse it. You can search the documents for a word or phase and find out how many times that word or phase is used in that document and so on.

You can open the index bag and browse it to find out what nodes you have created, the names you have given those nodes and how you have defined each node. You can organise the nodes into a system whose shape shows the ideas you are exploring and questions you are asking.

To be able to retrieve the bits of documents which are about a node, you have to draw a connection or series of connections between the index system and the document system. This process of "drawing connections" is a coding process.

You can get N4 to do coding, or you can do it yourself. The program will code for you every find of a word or phase you search for, or information you give N4 in a table. This automated coding can quickly accomplish repetitive tasks.

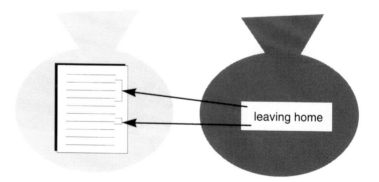

**The document and index systems with a connection
drawn between a document and a node "leaving home"**

In traditional or manual methods of coding the researcher decided which bits of a document related to a category, copied those bits and physically placed them inside the category container. This often meant lots of copying and cutting and filing cabinets (or shoe boxes!).

In N4 you can code much more swiftly and richly because you can work with text on the screen. Moreover, the boxes are not needed because only a reference to that bit of the document is stored at the node or category—not the actual texts.

If you want the actual text segments coded at a category—in our diagram depicting the "Big Bag Project" all the bits of documents that the category "leaving home" is pointing to—N4 retrieves the relevant bit of text from the document system and shows you these text segments on screen.

In N4 this process of viewing text on screen is called browsing. You can browse together all the segments of text coded at a category. While browsing you can think about them, re–code them, go back to the context and explore them again.

While the figure representing the links between the document and index systems shows one document and one node, in a project there are many documents and many nodes and *a piece of text may be coded at many nodes*. Indeed, if you are working in N4, there is no limit on how many categories a segment of text can be coded at—it should be coded as many times as it deserves!

If the text is about "leaving home" *and* a sense of "loss of identity", and we code where each is being considered, we can explore the relationships between these categories in the data.

In our project *Getting On* we were keen to understand how people from a range of living environments made decisions about changes in those context. We were also seeking to understand

differences in how people expressed a sense of personal autonomy and well being, and if these "expressions" were linked to
how they approached decisions to change their context. Did it
make any difference? How? How did people explain or recon-
struct what they had done?

In N4 you able to explore the many meanings associated with a
concept and how this concept relates to others. The tools provided to do this are the Index Searches.

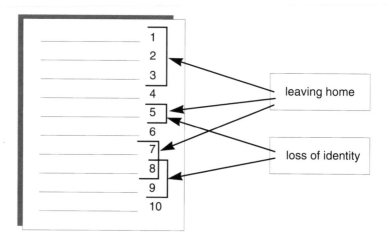

*A document where the interviewee talked of "leaving home" and
its relation to a sense of "loss of identity"*

N4 is able to search the index system for patterns of categories.
The type of relationship between the categories can be defined
by the search that you ask N4 to run. For instance an "Intersect"
search of the index system can retrieve bits which are categorized at "leaving home" *and* at "loss of identity". N4 will
retrieve from the document system text which is coded at both
categories, but not just one or the other.

In the diagram above, this would find only segments 5 and 8. This search is one of seventeen ways N4 offers for asking questions about patterns of coding. Using these, you can ask questions about subtle patterns of coding, and build on the answers by asking more questions.

2.5 Defining what is a "bit" for coding and getting back text	We have explored how the document and index systems relate to each other and the process of drawing connections between these two systems through coding. During the coding process a "reference" to a bit of a document is stored at the node for the relevant category.

If I were coding using a highlighter I would colour the passage of text that I was interested in—it may be a word, a phrase, a sentence, parts of lines or paragraphs. Using the computer, I can leave the document clean and just record a pointer, so long as I can identify *which* bit of the document is to be referenced at the node.

I do this by pointing to numbered text units. A text unit is the smallest bit or segment of text that N4 will recognise as a unit. How big or how small you make that segment is largely up to you. The size of the text unit determines the fineness of coding that you are able to do and the bits of text you can retrieve.

Within an imported document text units are numbered sequentially by N4 from the beginning to the end of the document. If a document is external, you choose a sensible unit (for example, "a page") and tell N4 how many text units are in the external document.

For imported documents, N4 recognises paragraph marks (hard returns) as the demarcation between one text unit and the next. This means you can easily automate marking segments of text which can be more easily separated by paragraph returns.

The most often used text units are lines or paragraphs. Some projects also use words or sentences. Choose your unit according to your requirements for coding and retrieval. There is no right or wrong size for a text unit. But most researchers find one that works for them. If you are unsure, import two copies of a document (with different names) in two formats—for example, one with lines and the other with paragraphs as text units. Code them taking note of how *you prefer to code* and the *fineness or resolution of detail* that you want to point to and retrieve.

2.6   Where do your growing ideas go?

As your ideas about your data develop, you need safe places to keep them and ways of keeping track of them.

Researchers using different methods use memos in different ways. Many researchers use notebooks, loose sheets of paper or the margins of transcriptions to record their thinking and ideas.

N4 won't mind if you continue to do so (you might code notebooks as external documents). N4 offers three ways of storing and growing ideas—in memos, which can be at nodes or documents; in annotations to documents; and in further documents appended to documents in your project.

In N4 the memos provide a distinct space where you can go to write about your thinking and ideas. They can be referred to, and added to, browsed and reported on. Memos can also be integrated into the project as data and worked with using the tools provided in the index and document systems.

Using memos early in your project means that writing is very much a part of the research process from the beginning of the project—when ideas are still simple and awkward—rather than at the very end, when the deadline is driving the writing rather than the development and expression of ideas and understanding.

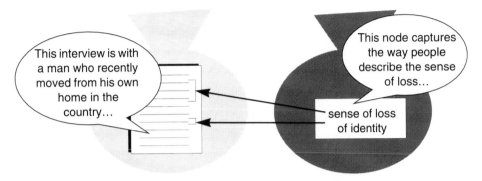

**The document and index systems showing
memos linked to a document and a node**

Memo–ing as a research tool can provide a space inside a project where thinking about data can also be less structured; less concerned with logic and sense; or the need to make sure your ideas are "really in the data". It provides an opportunity where thinking creatively can be stimulated rather than bound down to the constraints of deciding "does this bit belong in this or that category".

N4 codes any text units you nominate as annotations. When you insert a text unit in a document, you can ask for it to be coded as an annotation. They are a way to integrate your commentary into the body of the text, where it is most relevant, and code it. You can ask for all, or just some, of your annotations at any stage.

It is important to remember that an annotation is a "text unit" and is not intended to hold lengthy commentary.

You can append one document to another which is already in your project, rather than importing it as a new document. Appended documents can be used to record your thinking about a document or later reflections on a document. Because they are imported into N4 they can be coded at categories and their text can be searched and retrieved. For example your notes on an interview can be written up, then appended to the interview document.

This chapter has of course, not fully described the tools available in N4. But it provides a framework on which we will continue to build throughout the book. The next chapter explores setting up a new N4 project. If you have not already installed N4, now is the moment. Installation instructions are provided in the *Installation &Setup Guide* that comes with the software.

3
SETTING UP A N4
PROJECT

The steps which are required to create a new project in N4 are few and simple.

A N4 project can be set up relatively late during research. But like any tool kit, the software will be best used by those who know what it can do, and prepare their materials to use it. And almost always you will get most from the tools if you start using them early.

For those of you who are creating a new project with relatively few bits, the simple act of telling N4 to create a new project can also be helpful in forming commitment and clarity about your project. This leap is metaphoric or conceptual—it doesn't fundamentally change the bits, but rather enables you to conceptually hold the bits together and call it "a project".

There is also something immensely comforting in being able to get up from the computer after creating a new project, see it sitting snugly in its own directory or folder, pat it fondly, and feel that you have taken a giant step forward—for the project and qualitative research. The veneer, I admit, is a little thin, but with a few data documents and an embryonic index tree there is a definite sense of forward movement.

Using dialogue boxes

A dialogue box is like conducting a conversation with the computer. It is usually telling you something, or asking you to choose from the presented options what you would like to do next. While some are clearer than others in the way they visually communicate *what you are meant to be doing next*, they all need to be responded to in some way —don't ignore it or hope it'll go away. Read it, work out what the display is trying to communicate to you, and join in the dialogue.

3.1 Creating a new project

N4 is installed, but the application is not open. Locate where you installed the software (the folder or directory) and open up the folder (double click on it) so that you can see the N4 application icon—it looks like a tree.

Step 1: Double click on the N4 application icon to launch the application.

N4 opens a dialogue box which is asking you what you want to open.

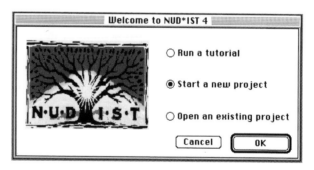

Step 2: Click on the radio button ● Start a new project. Then select OK.

Remember if a button in a dialogue box is highlighted with a heavy black outline you can also press Enter or Return to activate the command.

If N4 was already open, you can create a new project from the menu (at the top of the screen). Select Project, then choose New Project.

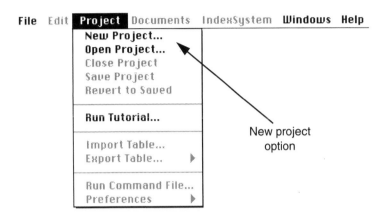

New project option

N4 will then guide you through a series of dialogue boxes as it sets up the project.

Step 3: This dialogue is asking you 2 questions—what name do you want to give to your project? and where do you want to save your project on the computer?

Navigate to the folder where you are saving the project

Type the name of your project here

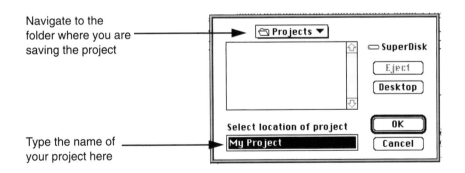

In the highlighted box type the name of your project where it says "My Project".

(Remember, if an area is highlighted, just start typing and you will replace what is there with what you type.)

N4 provides a folder called Projects, and will go there first to save the project. If you put your projects in this folder they will be listed whenever you select Open Project from the menu.

If you want to organise your projects differently, it is useful to create a new folder before asking N4 to create a new project, and then simply save your project into this folder.

PC users note: your screen display of this dialogue box may be slightly different, depending on what version of windows you are running. This dialogue box, on both platforms, operates like an "Open" or "Save" dialogue box for your platform.

Step 4:   This dialogue is asking you to type the project user's name. This may be your name or the name of your project team. Type a name, then click OK.

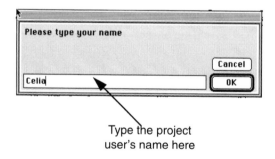

Type the project
user's name here

N4 creates the project and opens up two window displays—the *Node Explorer* and the *Document Explorer.*

The left hand side of both Explorer windows shows you what nodes or documents are already in the project. So far, you have imported or added no documents, and as yet created no nodes.

The menu reflects the
two system structure within N4

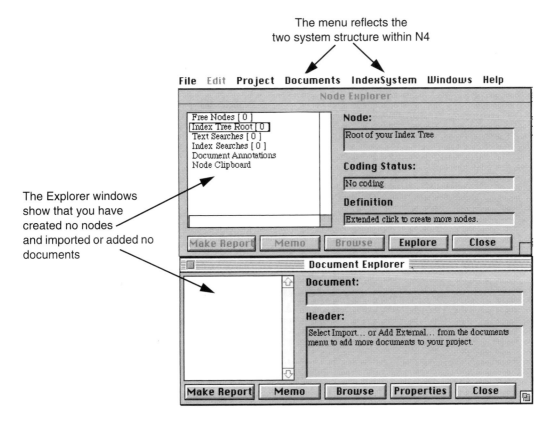

The Explorer windows show that you have created no nodes and imported or added no documents

Your new project is now set up and you can begin working with data. Some people begin by importing data documents, setting up an index system and browsing, reflecting on, and coding the documents. Others begin by making a few nodes for concepts they are exploring and writing memos.

But first, check what the software has done in response to your New Project request!

3.2 What's inside the project folder or directory

When N4 creates a new project it creates a project folder or directory inside of which there are five items. You can see these by selecting from the menu File, then Open. N4's editor will show you the contents of the folder you gave your project's name to.

One item is the "Project startup" file. When you next want to open your project, you choose the radio button Open An Existing Project when you launch N4. Or from the menu select Project, then Open Project. N4 opens up the display below. If your project is not in the "Project's" folder, your Startup file will not be immediately shown in this list. Click on the button Browse and navigate to your project Startup and add it to the list. You then click on the Startup file for the project you wish to open, and click OK.

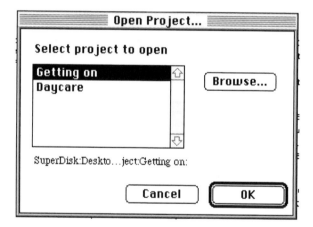

Alternatively, from the MacIntosh Finder or "MyComputer" Window in Windows 95, you can simply double click the Start-up file. It carries the QSR tree icon.

The Startup file can be renamed and given your project name.

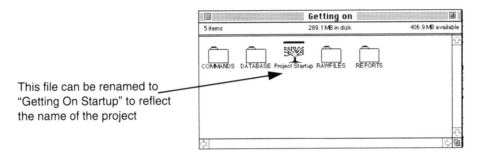

This file can be renamed to "Getting On Startup" to reflect the name of the project

There are also four folders inside the project folder:

- RAWFILES

- COMMANDS

- REPORTS

- DATABASE

The first three, RAWFILES, COMMANDS and REPORTS are not essential to the project, but provided for you to use as an inbuilt filing system. You can, if you wish, store the 'raw' data-files before they go into N4 in a folder which is different to your project's RAWFILES folder and simply navigate N4 to that folder to import files. In the same way you can store command files or save report files elsewhere on your computer and navigate N4 to where they are stored.

The DATABASE folder is *essential* to your project. In it are a series of files which hold all the bits of information about your index system and your document system.

This folder *should not be opened or changed* unless you are working under instructions from a QSR programmer. *The risk associated with opening and changing these files is that your project's database may be significantly corrupted or damaged.*

It is also essential to locate your project carefully. When you create a project, be sure you store it in the intended folder. N4 offers a "Projects" folder for all purposes. Never store a project inside another project's folder or in the N4 application folder!

3.3   Backing Up

It is also essential, as with any computer use, that you back up your project—*often!*

Since the database folder holds all the internal files, this is what you must back up. Copy the database folder, as you would copy any folder, using your operating system's 'copy' facility.

Make a copy of it on a *safe* medium. If you are spending long session working in N4 during a day, backup more than once a day. Much of what you are doing is creative conceptual work and it can be very difficult to recreate what is lost simply because you didn't take a break and make a copy of your database folder. (We've all done it!)

The next chapter covers the preparation of imported and external documents.

4

PREPARING DOCUMENTS

The N4 software is able to handle documents in two ways; imported or external. The actual texts of imported documents are made available to the computer inside N4. For external documents a reference to them is held in the computer.

Imported or External?

An imported data document might be a verbatim transcription of a taped interview or focus group; word processed responses to open ended questions, summaries of conversations or interviews, transcription of court proceedings or historical documents or down loaded text from the internet. Whatever the source and form of your data documents, to be utilised as imported documents they need to be created as plain text (or ASCII) files.

N4 is also able to handle *external documents*. For these only a reference to the data is held in the computer. This type of data may be books in a literature review, field diaries, archival material stored in a library; a collection of water jugs or photographs; or untranscribed audiotapes or video material. These types of data can be made available to N4 and integrated into a project through coding and memos.

4.1 Preparing document for importing

Before a document is imported into N4 it is saved as a plain text (or text) file. A plain text file is a file that has been saved without any special word processing formatting such as bolding, italics, tabulation or underlining. N4 will import any text in ASCII characters. This means that any characters which are created with the control, option or alt keys should not be used.

In plain text your document will look uniform, but of course upper or lowercase, paragraph breaks or line breaks are preserved. If you need to emphasise, highlight or delimit any words or notations in your document, use visual devices such as uppercase or bracketing.

N4 provides a text editor as part of its tool kit, but documents are usually prepared in a word processor to use facilities such as spelling check and word counts. Moving between the two applications can be speeded up significantly if a few simple routines are followed.

A document does not *have to* have any special preparation. If it is saved as text only, it will look like the document shown on page 27. In this document the smallest unit that N4 will recognise is a paragraph The unit is delineated by a hard carriage return (symbolised by ¶). The largest unit N4 will recognise is the whole document.

```
M ¶
I had to have an operation on my
eyes and that was a signal to
finish and of course with failing
sight it was difficult for me to
maintain the garden, look after
the house and my wife's health
was failing. She has this chronic
spinal complaint and one thing
and another...C [wife's name]
always said she would never leave
[street address] where we were
except in a box as she put it and
I felt we had to make a decision.
¶
Interviewer¶
Mmmm, did it take a lot of
persuading her? ¶
```

**A document saved as text only
with no header**

4.1.1 Writing headers

Any document can have a header. You can put it in and alter it at any time. When you get back all the material coded at a category or located by a text search, the headers will also be retrieved and will help you see where bits come from. When you list all your documents to review how your project is going, headers help you remember what they are!

If a data document represents an interview with a person, its header may contain information such as who was interviewed, the date of the interview, the identity of the interviewer, and other relevant information such as "interview was interrupted because someone rang the door bell".

The header simply contains information about the data document which is helpful in identifying it. Headers can be any length.

A header is not searched by N4 during any of its text searches. This means that *any information in the header which you wish to search for or to code using text searches* must be copied into the body of the text.

Entering headers in the rawfile

If you are importing the document, you can type the header into the rawfile. Just start any text unit you want in the header with an asterisk. N4 will recognise as the header all consecutive text units at the beginning of the document which start with an asterisk.

The header ends at the first text unit that does not start with an asterisk. Anything following the header is the body of the data document. The figure on page 29 shows a document with a header where each piece of information is a new paragraph.

Entering and changing headers for documents in the project

A document does not need a header. If you like you can simply add the header after the rawfile has been imported into your project. You can view, add and modify headers at any stage during an N4 project.

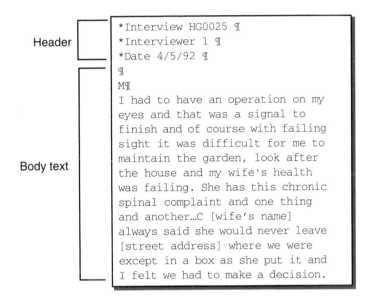

Header

```
*Interview HG0025 ¶
*Interviewer 1 ¶
*Date 4/5/92 ¶
```

Body text

```
¶
M¶
I had to have an operation on my
eyes and that was a signal to
finish and of course with failing
sight it was difficult for me to
maintain the garden, look after
the house and my wife's health
was failing. She has this chronic
spinal complaint and one thing
and another…C [wife's name]
always said she would never leave
[street address] where we were
except in a box as she put it and
I felt we had to make a decision.
```

***A header where each bit of information
is a new paragraph***

**4.1.2   Setting up
subheaders and
sections**

A subheader is a text unit in the body text of the document (that is, after the header has finished) that begins with an asterisk and ends with a hard carriage return. Subheaders do two things. They provide context for retrievals and divide the body text into sections. A section includes the subheader and all the text units following it until the start of the next subheader.

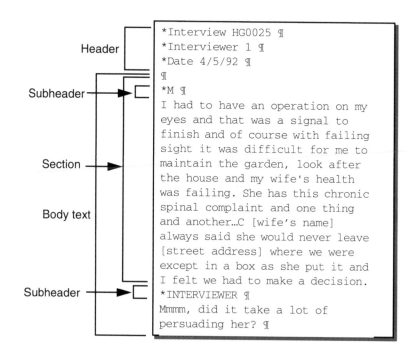

Header

Subheader

Section

Body text

Subheader

```
*Interview HG0025 ¶
*Interviewer 1 ¶
*Date 4/5/92 ¶
¶
*M ¶
I had to have an operation on my
eyes and that was a signal to
finish and of course with failing
sight it was difficult for me to
maintain the garden, look after
the house and my wife's health
was failing. She has this chronic
spinal complaint and one thing
and another...C [wife's name]
always said she would never leave
[street address] where we were
except in a box as she put it and
I felt we had to make a decision.
*INTERVIEWER ¶
Mmmm, did it take a lot of
persuading her? ¶
```

Subheaders provide structure to the
body of the data document

In the figure above the subheader identifies each speaker in the interview such as "INTERVIEWER "and "M" for a male respondent. A subheader could be used to identify the question number and text for the open–ended questions of a survey such as "Question 1: Are there other comments you wish to make".

A subheader provides context because it can be displayed with the text retrieved in reports of nodes or index searches, thus allowing the researcher to identify the text which relates to a question or who the speaker is for a piece of dialogue. This means that text is able to be related to the context from which it derived.

Subheaders provide substructure within the body of the data document. They are a way to mark a *bigger* bit of the text than the text unit. You can always ask N4 to show you that bigger bit.

Many projects can benefit from the use of this substructure provided by subheaders and sections. They can play a role in text and index searches and can be utilised in command files to automate coding processes.

4.1.3 Saving a word processed document as a plain text file

Your data document is ready to be saved as a plain text file. If you wish, it has its header and subheaders marked with asterisks. All you have to do is save the document in such a way that the carriage returns mark the text unit size you decided on. (Revisit "Defining what is a "bit" for coding and getting back text" on page 13.)

You can almost always get your word processor to put the hard returns automatically where you want them.

If you are using paragraphs as text units, the hard carriage returns are there already since it is how you mark the end of each paragraph. A warning to those typists amongst you (and there are plenty of you who do it) who press twice at the end of a paragraph—don't do it! Each paragraph return will be processed as a text unit and you will end up with many, many blank text units in all of your data documents. They will also be counted as part of a retrieval.

When you are preparing your documents turn on the display of white spaces and text symbols in your word processor so that hard carriage returns are displayed as a "¶". This will show you what will be the text units.

If you want sentences as units, use the search and replace in your word processor to insert a hard carriage return at the end of each sentence.

If you want lines, you have to save as a different format. Most word processors call this Text Only with Line Breaks. This places a hard return at the end of each line. So you want to be sure the line is not too long! If a line of texts exceeds 72 characters N4 simply wraps the left over characters to the next line—so one line will appear to be a line and a bit. It doesn't matter, but it looks silly!

A simple way to do this is when you are ready to save your document as text, select the whole document, change the font to Courier 10 point (so all characters take the same space), set your right margin to 12 cm (so no more than 72 characters are in a line) and then save as text only with line breaks.

The illustrations below show this process in Microsoft Word. There are many other word processors which may be used. Check the manual of the one you use to find out how to save a document as a text file. Most word processors provide the option of saving a text file with paragraph marks and line marks (these are hard carriage returns).

Step 1: From the File menu in Microsoft Word select Save As.

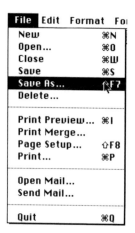

Step 2: The Save As dialogue is displayed. At the bottom of this display you can choose File Type. Click on this button and display the list of options that are available.

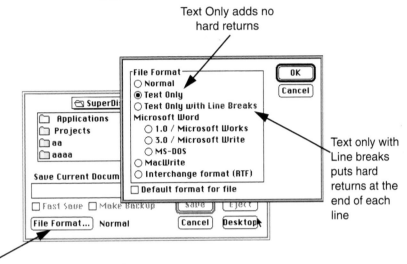

Text Only adds no
hard returns

File Format allows you to choose what
format a file can be saved as

Text only with
Line breaks
puts hard
returns at the
end of each
line

Step 3: If you want paragraphs as text units choose Text Only. If you want lines as text units choose Text Only with Line Breaks. Then click OK.

Step 4: Save the file in a sensible place! If you are using the filing system in your project folder, navigate to this folder and select the RAWFILES folder by double clicking on it.

Open the
RAWFILES folder
to save the text file
into this location
by double clicking
on it

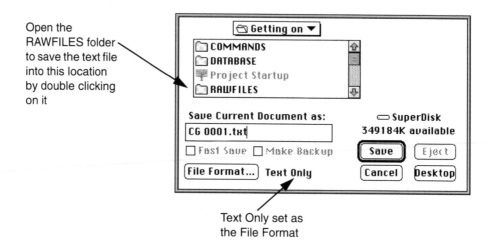

Text Only set as
the File Format

Step 5:   Give the file a name and then click Save.

Step 6:   Its a good idea to keep a backup of this file. N4 has copied it—so just move the file in RAWFILES to another folder.

In the next chapter we set up a document system in your N4 project. We will then import documents and add external documents to the project.

5

SETTING UP THE DOCUMENT SYSTEM

You are now ready to set up the document system. In this chapter we will import and append documents and add external documents to your project.

5.1 Importing raw files into the project

When a text file is imported, N4 recognizes the asterisks and hard carriage returns and formats the header, sub-headers and text units as you specified, and stores *a copy* of the document in its database.

The big moment has arrived. The first data document is ready to be imported. Your project is open with the two Explorer windows displayed.

Step 1: From the menu choose Documents and select Import.

N4 looks inside the RAWFILES folder (If your document is saved in another location navigate to where the file is stored.) The open window shows you all the files which are currently stored in the RAWFILES folder.

Step 2:   Click on the file you want to import, and then click OK.

Select the file to
import by clicking
on it

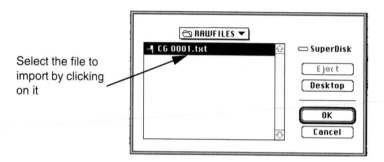

Step 3:   The next dialogue box is asking you what name you want the document to be known by in N4.

Notice that the document's current name is shown in the box (without its suffix). If you want the document to have a different name, overtype its name with a new one, then click OK.

N4 imports the document. Its name is now shown in the Document Explorer.

The selected document
is an on–line document

The title of the selected
document

The document
CG 0001 is
displayed in the
document list

Information that is
held in the header

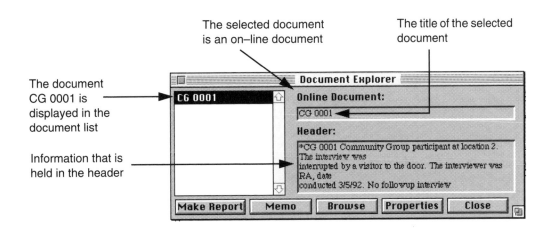

The Document Explorer is your direct access to data documents and information about them which is held in the document database. It displays a full list of documents in the project as a scrollable list, which is ordered alphabetically. If you select a document (by clicking on its title) the Document Explorer will also display information about the type of document it is and its header information. At the bottom of the Document Explorer you will find five buttons—Make Report, Memo, Browse, Properties and Close. By clicking on a button you are able to do any of these tasks.

To browse the text of a document, simply click on the title of a document in the list and click on the button Browse. The text of the document and a small palette adjacent to it is displayed. The palette lists options that you can use to view, code, examine the text and coding and make changes to the text.

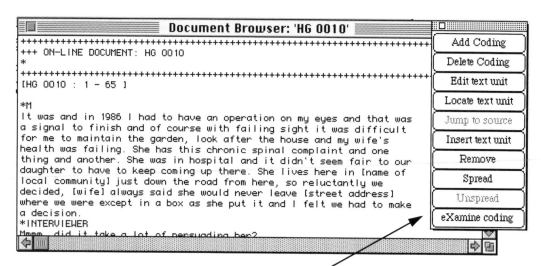

Palette of options available within the Browser.
The capital letter on each option can be typed as
a short cut to that option

In the Browser you are able to initiate any of the actions listed
in the palette by clicking on it or typing its keyboard short–cut
(the capitalised letter in each title).

5.2 Appending documents

A document may be attached as an appendage to another document which is already in your project, rather than importing it
as a new document. Appending a document means that it will be
added on to the original document. Its text unit numbers will
continue on from the last text unit number in the original document. Appending documents in this way enables related documents to be linked together as a continuous document.

An appended document, like an imported document, is a text
file copied into the database of your project.

Step 1: Choose Documents from the menu and select Append. N4 looks inside the RAWFILES folder (or navigate to where the file is stored). The open window shows you all the files which are stored in that location.

Select the file to append by clicking on it

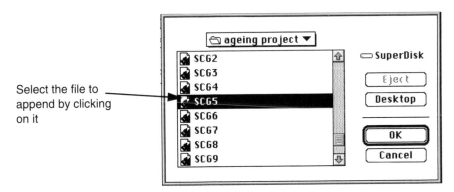

Step 2: Select the file you want to append by clicking on it, then click OK.

Step 3: N4 shows you a list of all the documents you have already imported. From this list choose a project document to append the new document to by clicking on it, then click OK.

Select the original project document to which you wish to append the new document

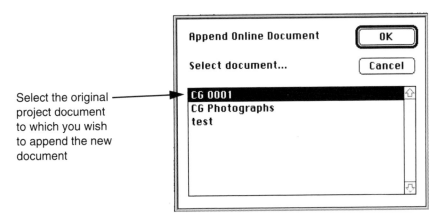

N4 imports the chosen document and appends it to the original project document specified. They are now one document.

5.3 Adding an external document to the project

External documents can be used for *any* data which is not imported into a project. They may be objects, images, tapes, film, documents which are unable to be recreated as text files or they may be text files you don't want to copy into your project (for example, large reports).

Often decisions also have to be made about the feasibility of converting data into suitable text files based on quality and cost involved.

To code or retrieve from an external document (just as from an imported document) you need to be able to refer to "a bit" or a unit.

These units are referred to as text units as for imported documents. But for external documents you can choose *what* a text unit may be, depending on the nature and structure of the data. For example: untranscribed audio tapes may use "a tape count" as a text unit; a collection of photographs may use "a photograph" as a text unit; or a book such as a a field notebook or a diary may use "a page" as a text unit.

Step 1: Choose Documents from the menu and select Add External.

Step 2: N4 opens a dialogue into which you type a title for the document, then click OK.

Type the title of
the document

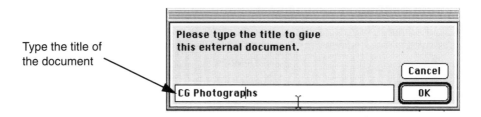

Step 3: You are then asked to enter how many text units are in this document. Type the number, then click OK.

Type the total number of text
units. In this document there
are15 photographs

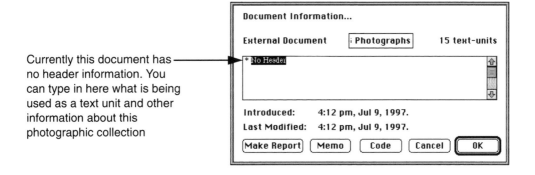

Step 4: N4 adds the document and opens the Document Properties display. You can add, if you wish, header information such as what is being used as a text unit. After you have finished modifying this window, click OK

Currently this document has
no header information. You
can type in here what is being
used as a text unit and other
information about this
photographic collection

Step 5: Close this display by clicking OK. The document is now a part of the list of documents in the Document Explorer.

The document CG Photographs is displayed in the document list

The currently selected document is an external document

The title of the selected document

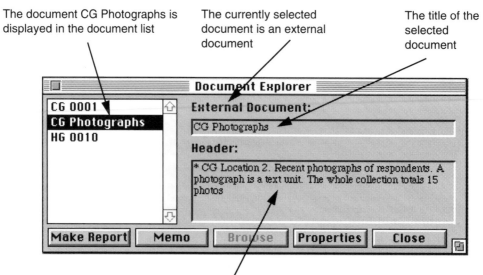

Information that is held in the header. This document's header now includes information about what has been defined as a text unit and what the collection holds.

5.4 Document properties and how to modify them

All documents have properties—they have a title and a header (which may be "No header"). These "properties" are given to documents by you when you import or add documents into your N4 project. You can edit and modify these properties at any stage in the project.

If you click on a document's title in the Document Explorer, you are able to see the document's properties displayed on the right hand side of the Explorer.

Step 1:   If you want to modify a document's properties, click on the button Properties.

Step 2:   The Properties dialogue box is displayed. By editing the title and header information you are able to modify this information in the database. Simply place your cursor in the title or header box and start typing. When you have finished modifying this display, click OK.

This tells you how many text units are in this document

The current title can be modified or replaced with a new title

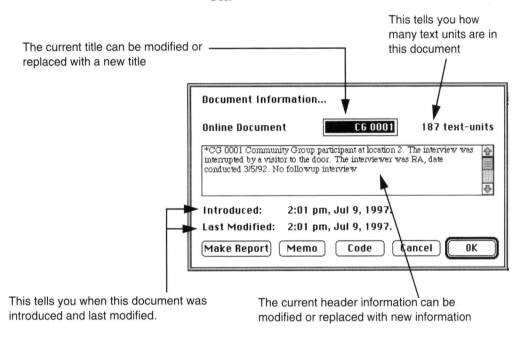

Document Information...

Online Document   CG 0001   187 text-units

*CG 0001 Community Group participant at location 2. The interview was interrupted by a visitor to the door. The interviewer was RA, date conducted 3/5/92. No followup interview

Introduced: 2:01 pm, Jul 9, 1997.
Last Modified: 2:01 pm, Jul 9, 1997.

Make Report   Memo   Code   Cancel   OK

This tells you when this document was introduced and last modified.

The current header information can be modified or replaced with new information

5.5 **Deleting documents from the project**

You may delete a document from the project. If you delete a document, you delete as well, *all of its coding*. Deleting a document can not be undone.

Step 1: Choose Documents from the menu and select Delete.

Step 2: Select the document you want to delete from the list by clicking on its name, then click OK.

Step 3: N4 will warn you that if you delete the document it and all its coding will be deleted and asks if you are sure you want do it. If you are, then click Yes.

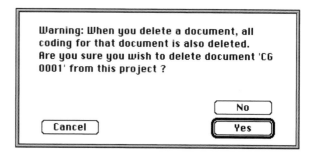

The next chapter explores ways to think and reflect on data. Once in N4 you can browse and reflect on the text of imported and appended documents and, if you like, review the data your external documents are referring you to. As you think and develop ideas about your data you can use memos and annotations to record them.

6

REFLECTING ON
DOCUMENTS

In N4 many opportunities are provided for you to reflect, revisit and review data and the way in which you are organising and structuring data through the index system. These tools provide ways to view data, link categories to data, make changes to data, and to store your emerging ideas about your data and categories.

In "Where do your growing ideas go?" on page 14 we talked about safe places to store your ideas as you reflected on documents. There are a variety of places that can be used in N4:

- you can insert your commentary into the body text by modifying a text unit;

- you can create an annotation;

- you can use memos;

- you can create a document in a word processor and append it to a project document; or

- you can use a note book and add it as an external document.

All of these tools offer you ways to interact with your data—to view it, to think about it and to record your thinking about it. This chapter explores tools for browsing and reflecting. The next chapters describe categorizing and coding.

6.1 Storing reflections by changing text units

The simplest way to store your reflections may be to edit the text, or insert a new text unit. You can, if you wish, make changes to the contents of a text unit by clicking on a text unit and then clicking on the option Edit text unit in the palette.

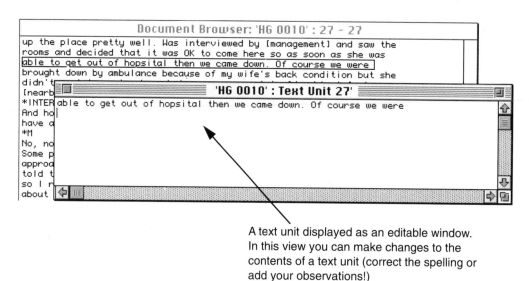

A text unit displayed as an editable window. In this view you can make changes to the contents of a text unit (correct the spelling or add your observations!)

N4 opens up the text unit as an editable window—you are able to change or add to the text unit. If you delete everything in this window, the text unit is not deleted, only its contents. It still exist in your document as a text unit and can be browsed, coded and retrieved!

When you have finished making changes, close the window and N4 will ask if you wish to save changes to the text unit. If you say "yes", the changes you have made are then saved into the document database.

Removing a text unit

You may wish to remove a text unit or units from a document permanently. If you do this, it and all its coding references are removed from the document database. The option in the palette to do this is Remove. (Remember, select text first!).

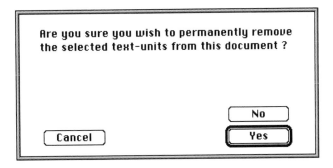

Click Yes, if this is what you wish to do. You can not undo this action!

6.2 Creating annotations

N4 supports annotating of a document. Annotations provide a way for you to insert into an imported document your commentary about the circumstances surrounding the text: an explanation of a change in direction within the dialogue; or your observations and feelings about the text; or a record of important contextual information such as nonverbal interaction, tonation and pausing. Extensive commentary about the document is probably best held in a memo.

Any text can be coded as an annotation. If an annotation is *an inserted text unit* N4 will code it for you. As a text unit the content of an annotation may be edited, removed or coded in the same way as any other text unit.

N4 provides a node "Document Annotations" at which any text units you wish to be an annotation can be coded. An inserted text unit will be automatically coded there when you create it, if you specify it is an annotation.

Since annotations are coded at a node, all N4's abilities to search patterns of coding apply. (For example, give me all my annotations in interviews with people living in retirement villages.)

Step 1: In the Document Explorer, click on the document's title, then click on the button Browse. In the Document Browser place your cursor in the text unit above which you wish to insert the annotation.

Step 2: In the Browser palette select Insert text unit.

Step 3: A dialogue is opened in which you are able to select what text unit properties you want the inserted unit to have. Click on the Document Annotation check–box, then click OK. (If this text unit was not an annotation you would select the text unit properties you wanted it to have and make sure the annotation box is unchecked.)

For an annotation make sure this box has a cross in it

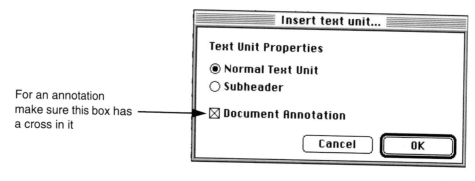

Step 4: An empty text window is opened into which you can type. When you have finished close the window.

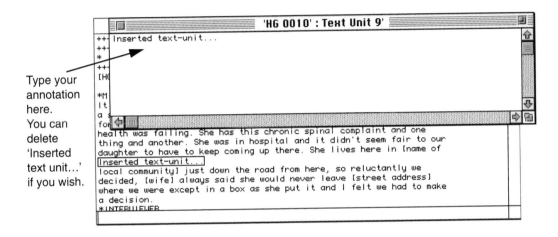

Type your annotation here. You can delete 'Inserted text unit...' if you wish.

N4 automatically codes the text unit at the node "Document Annotation".

In the Node Explorer the text of annotations can be browsed. The annotation we inserted into the document (and coded at the Document Annotation) is the only text coded at that node so far.

To browse all annotations you have created, click on Document Annotations in the Node Explorer, then click on the button Browse.

Each annotation will be displayed with its document title and header (if it has one)

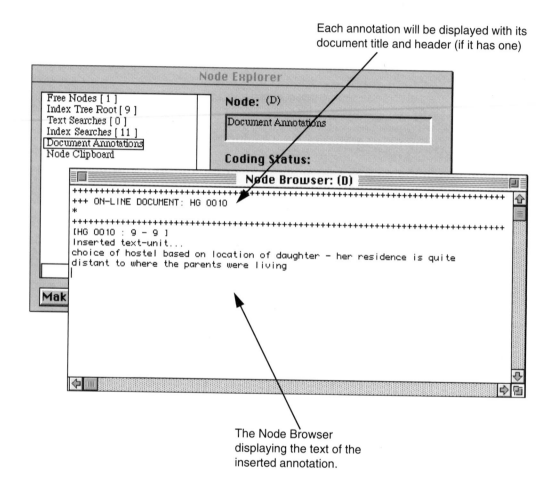

The Node Browser displaying the text of the inserted annotation.

6.3 **Attaching a memo to a document**

Memo–ing is a process that many researchers use to store their thinking and emerging ideas about data. In N4 a memo may be attached to a document or a node. A memo can be created, added to and modified at any stage in your project.

Step 1: Select the document by clicking on its title. Then click on the button Memo.

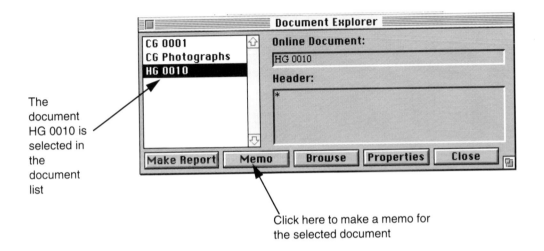

The document HG 0010 is selected in the document list

Click here to make a memo for the selected document

Step 2: This dialogue box tells you that there is no memo attached to this document and asks "Do you wish to create one?" Click Yes.

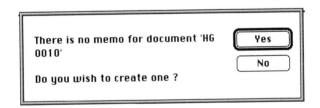

An empty text window is opened, and you simply start typing. You can, if you wish, time and date stamp your entry by choosing Edit then Insert Date & Time.

In this window you can edit, copy and paste, save and print. Other text formatting such as bolding and italics is not possible.

This entry has been time and date stamped

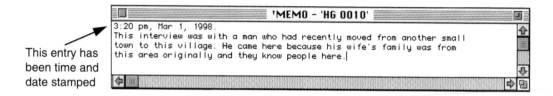

'MEMO – 'HG 0010'

3:20 pm, Mar 1, 1998.
This interview was with a man who had recently moved from another small town to this village. He came here because his wife's family was from this area originally and they know people here.|

If a memo is already attached to the document, N4 simply reopens the text window for you to continue memo–ing.

Step 3: After you have finished making your entry, close the window. N4 asks if you wish to save changes to the memo. If you do, click Yes.

It's now time to talk about ways to explore data. We do this in the next chapter.

7

EXPLORING DATA—
CATEGORIZING & CODING

In the end you can't get away from the inevitability that you will have to just sit there and do it! When all the cups of tea have run dry and the thought of more toast is not a turn on, it is time to turn to the data—and explore it!

This chapter is about the *processes of exploring* data—not about how to do it in N4. We talk about those tools in Chapter 8 (see page 65).

Qualitative data presents a number of challenges which researchers need to confront. These challenges are related to the nature of qualitative data—its lack of an explicit organising structure, its sheer volume (the thousand and one pages of transcription before you) and its specificity. They are also its intrinsic strength and beauty.

Somehow this specificity of data—the details about events, ideas, interactions, incidents—needs to be captured through analysis rather than diminished or reduced to such an extent that detail is collapsed into itself and represented by a few generic labels. On the other hand, if we don't do something about 'reducing' or conceptualising this specificity we are simply left with the mountain of transcriptions to read and re–read…and re–read if we are to understand and know each difference, each nuance, each aspect, each reflection which is part of our data.

7.1   Naming categories

Conceptualising data involves breaking down the data into discrete bits. These bits are closely studied and compared to each other to understand how they are similar and different and each discrete idea, event, interaction, incident is given a name. This name is a conceptual name and it represents a phenomenon.

Creating a name for a category or phenomenon says this category is distinct and palpable. At this category I am drawing together all those bits of data which are about a specific idea, event, interaction or incident. All those other bits are not! From this point I can start making statements about how it is related to all the other bits to which it has been compared. And I can start reflecting on the category, and developing it, rethinking it, breaking it into finer categories and linking them to bits of data. In this way, I structure and organise the data.

Many people engage in this process as a mental activity and leave writing it down until the end of the project. Writing down your thinking as you engage in comparing a piece of data or dialogue to another piece, can bring a sense of clarity or concreteness to the process and the categories which are created. In many ways the act of constructing sentences to communicate the concepts under study compels you to get clearer and sharper about what you mean. In many instances we not only sharpen but extend thinking through the writing. In the same way, seeing how the categories work as you link categories to data during the coding process continues to distil and develop the meaning associated with the category and continues the process of differentiating a category from other categories.

7.2 Where do names come from?

Most names for categories come from you. The name given to a category is usually the one that seems most logically related to the data it represents. When naming a category give it a name you can remember or one that is graphic enough to remind you what it is coding. Some researchers use words occurring in the text. These are called "in vivo" categories.

Other names for categories are drawn from literature, your own discipline or the description of the project itself. Many of these categories can be useful in the research context but it is important to re–examine them in terms of the data and how you are naming phenomena. It is very easy to assume or attribute an accepted meaning of a prepackaged category without questioning its relevance to, or utility in, naming the data. The overall effect can be of blocking or *jading* exploration rather than opening up, clarifying and *refreshing* analysis.

Categories, wherever their names came from, need to be thought about, developed and worked on. You need to be able to talk about the *meaning which you are attributing* to a category throughout the analysis process. Categories can undergo significant evolution throughout the life of a research project.

While categorization is not an arbitrary process, neither is it necessary to have a finite, unchanging list of categories or codes into which must be stuffed all the bits of data in this project!

The most important thing is to name a category so that you have somewhere to draw together all those bits of data and ideas which seem to relate to a phenomenon, to help you think about it. Don't feel "at a loss", overburdened or stuck because you can't come up with a catchy, "that's it" title. Give it a name and as the category develops a better name is usually found—as your understanding of the category becomes clarified and distilled.

People who get stuck at this point—"how do I go about naming what I see in my data?"—often decide they must need *more* data for it to start making sense! If you find yourself in this place, think again before dashing off into the nearest field! This process is not always an easy one, it takes lots of energy and persistence. At times it may even feel like you are taking a walk through knee deep, volcanic mud. Persist!

It can also be lots of fun.

7.3 Descriptive and conceptual categories

The categories that are created should reflect the data—name incidents, events, ideas, interactions. These categories will also reflect the researcher's view of the data. This does not mean that a category and how data is coded for that category reflects a pre-conceived view of what the data will mean. But rather, all the categories (the index system that is created for a project) reflect both the intention of the researcher (your research question) and the data. It is this frame through which the data is viewed which enables you to interpret data and conceptualise it in some way. The distinctions created through categorization should be meaningful in terms of reflecting the data. Reflecting the data doesn't mean that categories simply or only summarize or describe data. *Descriptive categories*, such as gender, age, group membership and so on may be useful. But *conceptual categories* involve a reflection of the data which the researcher brings through interpretation—and is a new view of the data.

So, the project's categories (the index system) is no mere *ad hoc* collection of labels which seemed reasonable at the time. Each category is created through a process of differentiation from and in relation to other categories. Each time we create a category we are making a decision about how to organise the data.

7.4 Dimensionalizing categories

Categories rarely stay the same as understanding grows. They can usually be further developed in terms of subcategories or dimensions. This process of dimensionalizing a category is a powerful process in that it facilitates a sharpening in thinking and enhances analytical development of a category—its meaning and association of meaning.

Naming a subcategory enables you to talk about the category: its dimensions or subcategories; the subcategories in relation to each other; the category in relation to its subcategories; and the category in relation to other categories.

In the project *Getting On* a phenomenon was identified which was named "Absolute Image of Old Age". We had noticed the way in which people, regardless of their age, seemed to have a view about what it is like be "old" (they were not there yet) or at the end of life. This phenomenon appeared to have two aspects: one is described in terms of diminishing metal capacity; and the other, diminishing physical capacity.

Exploring both of these aspects as distinct subcategories, we developed our understanding of not only the subcategories in themselves and how people expressed those aspects, but the relationship between these two subcategories, and the relationship of the subcategories to the category itself. This category was developed and mapped in terms of its relationship to other major categories which explored aspects which facilitated or blocked decision making about living environments.

What to do with the categories you develop, and how to link them to the data and ideas? Back to N4! The next chapter explores how you are able to create categories and link categories with data through coding. But first, an introduction to N4's nodes, and the ways they work for you in the crucial process of categorization.

**7.5   Nodes and where
they live in N4**

In Chapter 2 (revisit page 58) we explored the index system and spoke of it as being made up of nodes which may organized in a "tree" structure in the Index Tree, or managed as an unstructured list in the Free Nodes area. There are three other areas of nodes in the index system: Text Searches, Index Searches and Document Annotations.

All the nodes in the index system are displayed in the Node Explorer. In the Explorer the index system is shown as a list which looks and behaves similarly to a computer's folder/subfolder display. If your Node Explorer window is not open, go to the IndexSystem menu and choose Explore.

Clicking on an node area will show you a list of nodes in that area

An "!" beside a node title indicates it has a memo attached to it

If a node has a "+" beside its name it has subcategories below it. If there are no nodes below it a "–" will appear

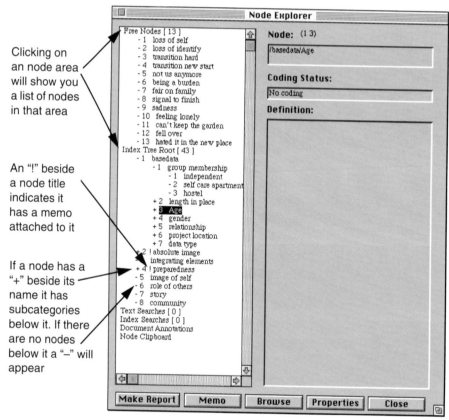

58

All nodes have numerical addresses and titles. A node's address reflects its position in the index system and it's title is its name (the name given by you to a category). Both of these can be changed by you at any stage. You can nominate a node address when you create a node. If you don't, N4 will simply use the next consecutive number available. You can tell if a node lives in the Free Nodes area because its address will have "F" as a prefix. Text Searches have a "T", Index Searches have a "I" and Document Annotations have a "D".

A node's address in the Index Tree reflect its structure:

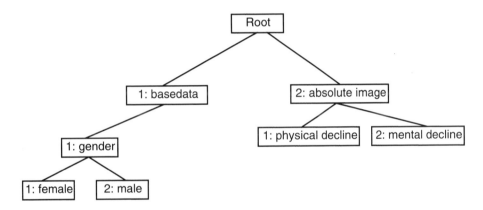

The Root has no address and is represented by empty parentheses "( )". The nodes immediately below the root are first level nodes, and theoretically represent the most general categories. A node can have subcategories below it. These are its children. All children of the same node are siblings of each other. The node above, to which it is attached, is its parent. The whole structure is called a subtree. The numerical address given to each node is unique and reflects these relationships.

In the Index Tree shown above the full address for the node absolute image is (2); physical decline (2 1); and mental decline (2 2). The first digit of a child node's address is derived from its parent's address, and the second digit reflects its place in the subtree. As you move down the tree, the addressing continues in the same way. Each node's address contains information about itself and, implicitly all its ancestors. So the address of the node "male" is (1 1 2).

The Index Tree can be displayed as a "Tree". To display the Index Tree go to the IndexSystem menu and choose Display Tree. (You are also able to display a duplicate of the Index Tree. The duplicate display can make shifting and merging nodes a lot easier!) To move around the tree click on the arrows to move to the next level or section of the tree. The small display in the left hand corner is a summary display which shows you an overview of the whole tree. The black band (currently at the top of this display) shows you where you are in the large tree display.

The Summary display showing you where you are in the tree

Use the arrows to move around the tree

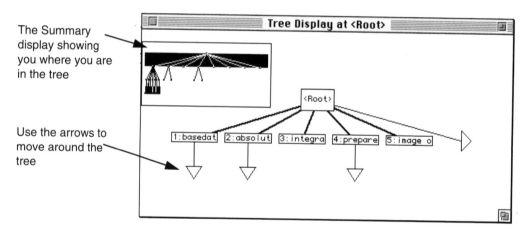

The Node pop–up menu shows the options that are available for working with nodes. This menu may be called up at any stage by pointing to a node and right mouse click (Mac users hold down the mouse button). This menu can be called up in the Tree Display or in the Explorer.

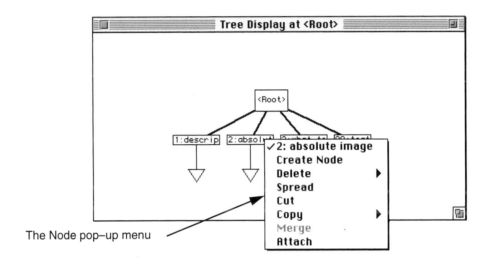

The Node pop–up menu

Creating a new node

Nodes may be created and modified within the Node Explorer or the Tree Display using the Node pop–up menu. You can create categories as you think of them while you browse a document, or you can create them "up front" before doing coding at them. We will create them up front first.

Step 1: To make a Free Node, point to that area. To make a node in the Index Tree, point to the node below which the new node will be attached and call up the Node pop–up menu.

Point to where the new node will be created:
Free Nodes
or
nodes in the Index Tree

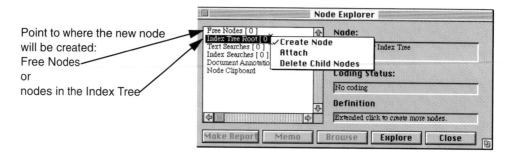

Step 2: Choose Create Node.

A dialogue box is opened into which you type a numerical address, title and a definition for the node you are creating. All nodes need an address and title. The definition is optional. The tab key can be used to move from frame to frame in this dialogue.

Node title   Node address "1"

Definition
of node

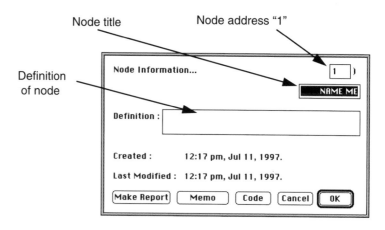

The node title field in the top right corner is highlighted, and says "Name Me". Type the name you want to give this category.

The address reflects the new node's place in the list of Free Nodes or within the Tree and is shown in the box above the title. If you wish, you can change the address simply by overtyping it.

Step 3:   Click OK.

N4 creates the node and it appears in the Node Explorer.

We are now ready to explore ways you can grow the index system and do coding in N4. In the following chapter we will examine ways to design and restructure the index system as the project progresses and undergoes review.

EXPLORING DATA—CATEGORIZING & CODING

8

LINKING CATEGORIES
WITH DATA—CODING

Part of the strength of working inside N4 is that it enables the researcher to move interactively between the data held in the document system and the concepts under exploration held in the index system. Central to the qualitative analysis process is the activity of creating categories *from* data, and linking categories *with* data through coding.

It is important to emphasise at this point that much coding, especially early in a project, involves creating the node to code at, rather than coding into a pre–existing scheme. The tools in N4 are designed to support this process of ideas emerging out of the data.

There are a number of ways this process can be approached in N4.

- Browsing and coding text on screen;

- Reporting on a document and marking up a paper copy with codes to be entered using a dialogue box; and

- Searching a document's text using string and pattern searches which may be incorporated into the index system as nodes.

All of these approaches enable you to create categories, to link them with data by storing at a node the references to text units of a document which you judge belong there. Throughout the coding process the index system is able to undergo continual revision as data transforms the meaning associated with a category.

The first two will be explored in this chapter and the third is presented as part of Chapter 11 on page 103.

8.1 Browsing and coding text on screen

In the Browser you are able to explore documents on screen by:

- viewing their texts and reflecting on them;

- creating categories at nodes; and

- coding the texts and viewing and revising coding.

N4 is designed for coding and creating categories interactively on the screen. It has an immediacy. It offers you a sort of closeness to your data and ideas; an ability to move quickly around them, check what else is coded at a category, rename it, add to its memo, edit in an annotation, or alter the document—all on the fly—whilst you are thinking about it.

The big advantage of coding on screen is that as ideas occur to you, they can be created immediately. See something in the text, just tell N4 to code it. And if it's a new category, just name it— the category is created and the coding done for you—while you go on getting excited by the next passage of text and your ideas about it.

You can also at any stage ask N4 what other nodes code this passage of text (click on the option eXamine coding in the palette) and go to those nodes to think about them. So, moving around your thinking and coding procedures at will.

Let's begin with an extract of dialogue. An elderly man is reflecting on the series of events and incidence which led up to the decision to move from his home to a retirement village. Let's read his dialogue and absorb what he is telling us.

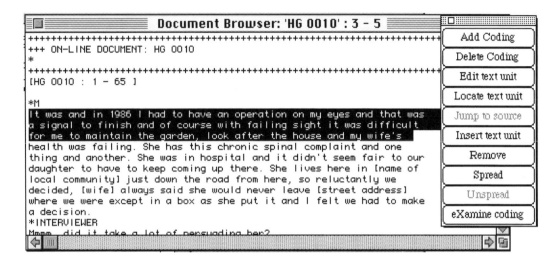

Perhaps we want to create a Free Node for "a signal to finish". Just highlight the text and tell N4 the idea. It makes the new category a node and does the coding. Or perhaps we should explore "chronic" and its many meanings—make a Free Node to remind you to think about that. Here's how.

Step 1: Select the document you wish to browse by clicking on its title. (Remember, you can't browse text of an external document!) Then click on the button Browse.

Step 2: Click and drag over the area of text you wish to code at a category. The area is highlighted.

Step 3: Click on Add Coding in the palette (or type an "A") to call up the Add Coding dialogue box.

If you do not know the address you can use Select to locate the node in the list, or to create a node where you want it

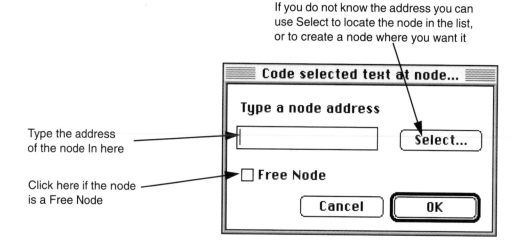

Type the address of the node In here

Click here if the node is a Free Node

Step 4: Tell N4 the node to code at. You can type the title of the Free Node you want to code at, or the address of the node if it is to go in the index tree, or you can select an existing node to code at.

If you type the address of a node that does not exist, or a title for a Free Node that does not exist, N4 will ask if you want to create that node.

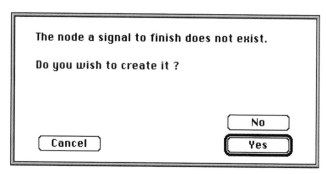

Step 5: If you say Yes, it will do so. (You are asked to give a title if you had provided just the address.)

Step 6: Or alternatively, you can use the Select button to choose an existing node, or create the node first (before coding at it using the Node pop–up menu). Then click Select.

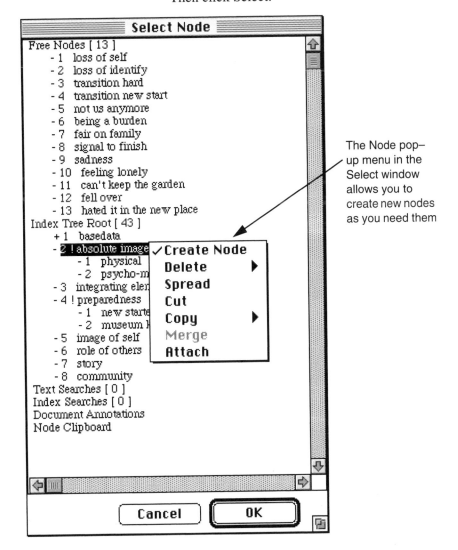

The Node pop–up menu in the Select window allows you to create new nodes as you need them

N4 inserts the node's address (or title if it's a Free Node) into the Add Coding dialogue box.

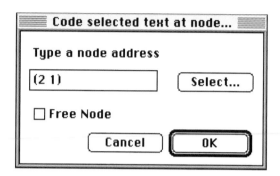

Step 7: Now click OK and N4 adds the text unit references (of the highlighted range) to the selected node.

To add the next code hit "A" again and so on. You'll find now you know the routine it's very fast.

8.2 Coding off the computer, then entering coding later

Maybe you want to be released from the computer? You can do coding without have the text on the screen, by simply telling N4 which units to code where. Coding using this approach allows you to leave the screen and use a paper report of the data.

You can make a report of an imported document showing the text unit numbers and print these. These printed reports can be marked up with codes noted alongside bracketed text unit ranges.

Working in this mode means that you can mull over the data under a tree, on the train or in bed. Later, when you return to the computer, these codes are added to N4 through a dialogue box in which node addresses and text unit ranges are specified.

We often begin coding using reports because the margins can be used to scribble and jot as we try to orientate to the data and begin to articulate categories or thematic areas. Initially, this process of conceptualising (unknown) phenomena can feel awkward. We find the reports offer a freedom to explore and brainstorm new ideas.

Try it! Find the process that suits how you work. The different options simply provide alternative interfaces from which you can choose.

8.2.1 Setting where text unit numbers are shown

Before you make a printed report, you might like to change where text unit numbers will appear. Most people want them on the right margin. If you don't (you may not want any) you can change settings. Here's how.

Step 1: From the Project menu choose Preferences, then Line Numbering.

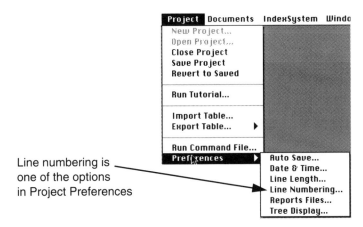

Line numbering is one of the options in Project Preferences

Step 2: Click on the margin you would like the text unit numbers to print in, then click OK.

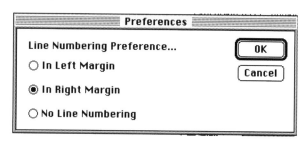

8.2.2 Making a report of a document

Step 1: In the Document Explorer, select the document by clicking on its title. Click on the Make Report button.

N4 opens up a dialogue box inside which you can choose what parts of a document's *text* and *coding* information you wish to report on.

The Document Explorer sitting behind the Make Report dialogue box

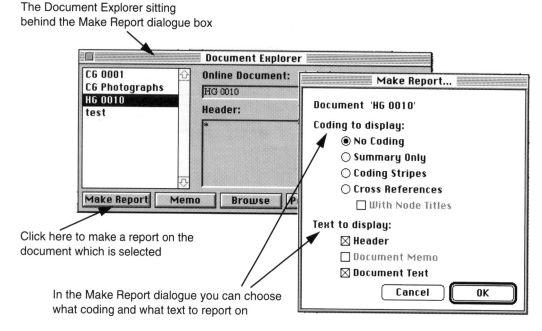

Click here to make a report on the document which is selected

In the Make Report dialogue you can choose what coding and what text to report on

Step 2: In Coding to display, click on No Coding. This means that no code references will be reported.

Step 3: In the Text to display section, click on Header and Document Text. This means that all of the document including its header will be reported. Then click OK.

Step 4: N4 will open a dialogue in which you can specify the text unit range for a document you wish to have reported. The default is the entire range in the document. For our purposes here, we want the whole document so this dialogue remains unchanged. Click OK.

```
Make Report...                         [  OK  ]

Select text unit range for report      [ Cancel ]


From: [0]          To: [244]
```

N4 retrieves the document from its database and shows it on screen with text unit numbers as you preferred. You can print, save, edit or discard this report as you need to. It is a report out of N4, so any changes you make won't change the document in the database.

Step 5: From the menu select File and choose Print. Make the necessary responses to the Print dialogue, then click Print.

Very large reports will not be able to be printed directly from N4. These reports will only be displayed in N4 as a "read–only" format and can be saved to file. (The Save option is located in the File menu.) Once you have saved the report, these reports can be opened and printed from your word processor. If you want the formatting to look the same as in the N4 report, set the document's font to Courier 10 point before printing. You will find that the text unit numbering will realign itself.

8.2.3 Making a list of nodes

You can also list all the nodes (or part if you wish) in the index system. This list can be referred to as you jot codes alongside passages of text on your report.

Step 1: From the IndexSystem menu, choose List Nodes.

Step 2: N4 opens up a dialogue box in which you can choose which part of the index system you would like to list and data for each node and document. The default is set on all of the tree with no other data retrieved from the index system. After you make your choice of what to list, Click OK.

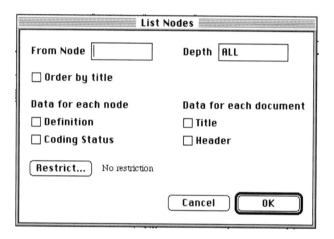

8.2.4 Recording coding on a printed report

The next step is to go for a walk to the local park or garden and sit under a tree! You need to have at hand the reports of the documents you want to code, a current list of nodes, something to write with, and maybe a notebook and lunch. (Leave the novel on the library shelf—it will be too distracting!)

This part of the process is similar to browsing on screen except that you are browsing a paper report. What you are doing is creating categories to represent what you discover as you read, and together with categories already created in the index system, linking these categories to data through noting codes against text unit ranges. The diagram below shows one way to mark up a report. The bracketed text units have node addresses written beside them if categories already exists. Those brackets with titles beside them are new categories and will be entered as free nodes. You can develop your own methods. It is shown here as an example of one way only.

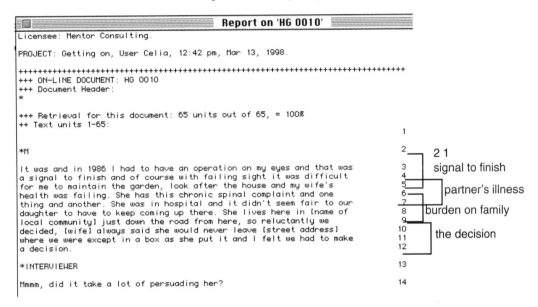

If your document is external (for example a book, your diary, a heap of photographs) create a way you *like* for noting what 'text units' of that document (pages, numbered photos etc) should be coded at which nodes.

You are now ready to enter the coding into N4.

8.2.5 Entering coding from a paper report

Step 1: From the menu choose IndexSystem and select Add/Delete Coding.

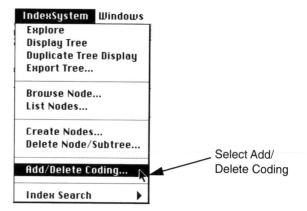

Select Add/Delete Coding

N4 will open up the Add/Delete Coding dialogue in which you type text unit ranges to be coded at a node.

Step 2: Click on the Select button adjacent to the Document Name box. Select the document you wish to code, then click OK.

Step 3: Working from your marked up report, type in or use the Select button to choose existing nodes, or create new nodes, as you need them.

Step 4: Press the tab key to move down to From Text Unit—To Text Unit boxes. From your report read the first text unit number and the last, and type them in here. Use the tab key to move from box to box.

If your text unit range is only one text unit type in the text unit from itself to itself. If you want to code all of the units in this document at the node, click Entire Document.

Type the text unit range in these boxes

Or you can choose to add coding to the entire document

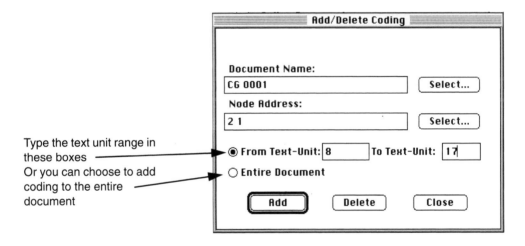

Step 5: Click Add or press Return or Enter.

Step 6: Continue entering coding until you have finished. Then click on Close.

The next chapter explores ways in which you can review and think about your categories, and redesign your index system, as the project progresses.

9

CRAFTING THE INDEX SYSTEM

N4 supports the process of categorization and coding in a very straight forward manner. Many of the tasks, which without the aid of computer software were formidable, have become nearly too easy. With N4 data can be radically reorganised; codes can be split and merged, duplicated and deleted; and as well, undergo conceptual change relatively simply and quickly.

We've looked at how categories get created from data during coding. But there are many ways of creating them—and they have many purposes. We now want to start viewing and arranging them as the project progresses.

Categories may be created at any stage in a project's life. When a category is created it may be part of a subgroup of categories, or its position in the overall structure of the index system may not be yet known. If its place within the overall index system is known the new category can be created as part of the tree. If not, it can be created as a Free Node which can be later moved into the tree as the category, and its relationship to other categories, takes shape. Other categories are created to hold ideas (rather than coding)—these ideas can be stored in a memo or the node itself is a "conceptual bridge" which pulls together a cluster of categories.

9.1   Re–organising categories

The index system can be continually added to, reorganized and restructured throughout analysis. The ability of the index system to remain fluid and flexible throughout analysis means that you are able to continue to pursue emergent understanding of the data and not jettison the process because it got "too hard" or clumsy.

Being able to make changes to the structure of the index system means that you are able to metaphorically "cut–up" the data in a different way. When you shift, combine or delete a node the coding references to the documents are automatically updated to reflect the changes that you have made.

9.1.1   Shifting a node or subtree to a different place

Shifting a node or a group of nodes enables you to restructure or reorganize the categories to reflect changes in relationships and emergent relationships between nodes.

In our project *Getting On* we initially created a number of Free Nodes which were about some sort of "loss": loss of identity; autonomy all gone; no longer us; left behind things that were us. These codes were later moved into the Index Tree and re–grouped under a more general category "sense of loss".

More specific categories can be moved below a more general category; categories from different parts of the system can be moved and grouped together as their relationship to each other becomes apparent; new more general nodes can be created to group together clusters of nodes; or nodes can be moved in and out of the "free" zone to meet the ever changing needs of analysis.

Free or Tree nodes can be rearranged by changing the order of nodes. They can be attached or merged into other parts of the index system. Tree nodes can also be shifted collectively, by moving subtrees.

Shifting nodes means that you are also shifting all the coding stored at a node or in a subtree.

In the schema below there are two main ideas represented by clusters of nodes. One cluster—the "basedata" subtree—*holds information* about participants in the project. In our project *Getting On* a number of nodes, like gender, were created to hold information and included nodes for age, type of living environment, year of the project and type of data (for example, interviews, group discussions). The other cluster of nodes—the "absolute image" subtree—represents a *concept being explored* in the project. These nodes, and others like it, are conceptual nodes rather than information holders.

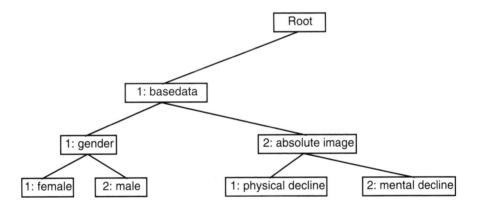

To differentiate these two distinct subtrees, the tree will be reorganised by moving "absolute image" and its subcategories out of the category "basedata" and placing it below the root as a distinct subtree. The new schema is shown on page 83.

Step 1: Select the node you wish to shift by clicking on its title. We are moving a subtree, so we select the node which is the *parent* of the subtree.

Step 2: Call up the Node pop–up menu. Choose Cut, then choose Subtree from the list.

To move absolute image and physical decline and mental decline, select absolute image and cut

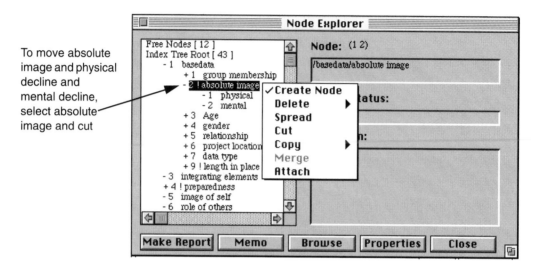

Step 3: Next we select the node to which you wish to attach the subtree by clicking on it. Call up the Node pop–up menu and choose Attach.

Step 4: N4 queries whether this is the right move. If it is, click Yes. N4 attaches the subtree below the selected node.

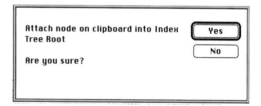

The nodes that have been shifted are unchanged except they now hold a different place in the overall index system and their addresses reflects this shift—(2) "absolute image; (2 1) "physical decline"; (2 2) "mental decline". The coding at each of these nodes is untouched. (Check by browsing one!)

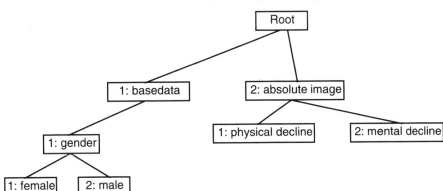

Shifting a node or a subtree reflects the ongoing reorganization of categories and data throughout analysis. The relative ease with which this can occur means that categories and their coding can be reviewed and radically reorganised quickly and comprehensively, without the need to start at the beginning of the coding process.

9.1.2   Combining categories

Moving nodes is only one way of thinking about them. What if we wanted to think differently about "decline"—browsing *all* the text on physical or mental decline and making new, subtler categories about "absolute image".

To do this nodes can be merged, so that what may have been two or more categories are now one. Merging nodes together means that the coding at one node is added to the coding at the second node. If common coding is at both nodes these text unit references are not duplicated—N4 merges them seamlessly.

You can merge any number of nodes, but it is done one at a time.

Step 1: Select the node you wish to merge into another node. Call up the Node pop–up menu and choose Cut.

Step 2: Click on the node you wish to merge into. Call up the Node pop–up menu and choose Merge.

The node is now part of the node into which it was merged and shares its title, address and definition.

In the schema below (2 3) "frailty" is merged with (2 1) "physical decline" and "frailty" as a distinct category will be deleted.

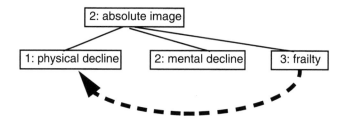

9.2 **Changing a node's properties**

Changing the name of a category

Changing the name of a category by editing the title of a node in the Node Information dialogue seems almost trivial in its simplicity. Within the context of your analysis the modification or change in the name of a category is symbolic of your changing understanding of a category and its essence. In this context, changing a category by re–naming it becomes a powerful analytical process in itself. It also enables the Index Tree to remain fluid thus enabling ongoing regeneration of the nodes as analysis continues.

Step 1: In the Node Explorer select the node, then click on the Properties button.

The Node Information dialogue box is opened, with the title highlighted. Start typing and the new title will replace the old.

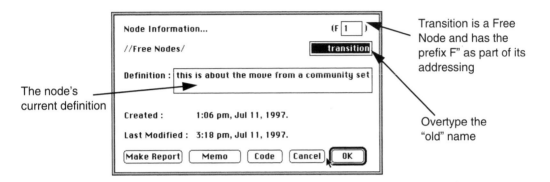

The node's current definition

Transition is a Free Node and has the prefix F" as part of its addressing

Overtype the "old" name

Step 2: Click OK.

Giving a category a definition

While N4 will allow a node to be created without a definition. Explicitly using this facility can play a beneficial role in the analysis process. Recording a definition compels you to be clear about what a category is trying to capture. Writing it down not only means you have to construct a meaningful description of the category, but it also provides a record of the definition.

Making explicit the ongoing defining process which is part of analysis has multiple benefits. First, it allows you to refer to the definition as coding progresses to ensure consistency in the interpretation of a category. This can be useful over time and within a research team to ensure consistency of coding. Secondly, as the definition of a category changes, the definition can be copied into the node memo (and date recorded) to record changes in the definition over time. (To attach a memo to a node, click on the node's title and then click the Memo button.) This allows the researcher to map the evolution of a category as understanding and construction of the category changes.

You can type the definition when you create the node. Or at any time you can write or alter it by selecting the node in the Node Explorer and clicking on the button Properties.

9.3   Deleting bits from the project

Initially most people want to know how to get things into a NUD•IST project. But there are many times (and surprisingly soon!) in a project when you will want to delete bits, especially during periods of review. The delete option in the Node pop–up menu provides a range of things that you may wish to delete: nodes, a node's children, coding and memos. The process for deleting all of these things is identical. Here we will work through the process using a node.

Step 1:   Select the node by clicking on its title in the list.

Step 2:   Call–up the Node pop–up menu and select Delete, then choose an option from the list.

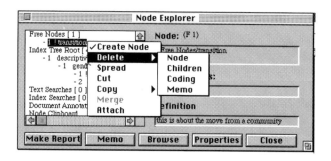

N4 gives you a warning about what you have asked to do. (Remember there are no undo's!)

In this case a node is being deleted.
N4 identifies the node by its address and title

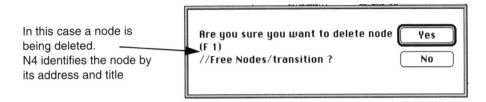

Are you sure you want to delete node (F 1)
//Free Nodes/transition ?

Yes

No

Step 3: If this is what you want to do, click Yes.

Deleting a node

It is advisable to review categories periodically. During analysis some prove only transitory—they were created for a specific phase in the analysis and are no longer required. These categories can be removed permanently from the index system.

Deleting a node means that the node, and all of its coding are removed from the project. If there are nodes attached below the node which is deleted, these nodes and all of their coding are also deleted. This action can not be undone.

Deleting the Children of a Node

The children of a node are all the subcategories attached below a node. If you delete the children of a node, the node itself is not removed from the project. All of "child" nodes and their coding are removed.

Deleting all the coding held at a node

Alternatively, you may wish to retain a category in the index system but want to purge all the coding held at the node. This empties a node of coding. This process is different to deleting coding through the Node Browser where coding is deleted from the selected text units in a document. Deleting coding at a node will delete all references for that node.

Deleting the coding of "absolute image " removes all the references held by the node but the node itself is not deleted.

(You can check that it has "worked" by clicking on its title in the Node Explorer and you will see that its Coding Status has changed to "No coding".)I

Deleting a node's memo

The node's memo is simply removed from the project. This does not affect the node itself.

In the next chapter we will explore Interactive Browsing as we continue to our process of moving in iterative cycles between data and thinking about data.

10

INTERACTIVE BROWSING

In Chapter 6 (revisit page 45) we explored the tools which are available in the Document Explorer to browse the text of documents. In this chapter we will continue this exploration and look at the ways in which you are able to move from Document Browser to Node Browser and back again, as we explore data in a range of contexts—the whole document, a node, the section within which the coding occurs, a segment of text and other coding.

The ability to jump from browser to browser enables you to work interactively between index system and data and to see instantly the outcomes of any changes you make in the project. Through the Browsers you are able to develop categorization of data, and to explore, review and revisit data. On each visit you can, if you wish, conceptually re–frame the data through re–coding or modifying the index system. This means that data once coded *doesn't have to stay coded or coded in the same way*. Coding is able to stay liquid or fluid for longer because we have the tools to change it (and it won't add another two years to your research project!).

This quality of "liquidity" enables you to continue to clarify and distil a category, and what is coded at it, for as long as you need to. It also brings to the process a sense of playfulness and risk taking—so you can keep asking questions of your data and categorization.

The palette lists the tools which are available in the Browsers.

palette of tools

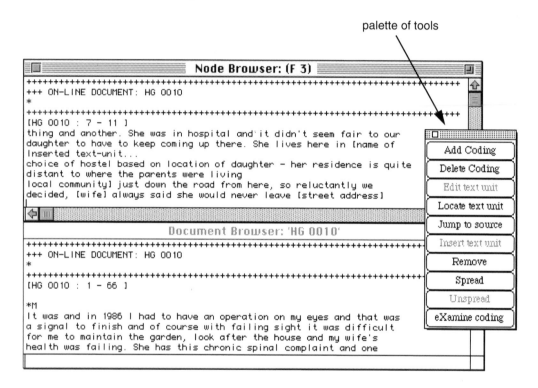

Palette options and their effects change depending on the context—are you in the Document Browser or the Node Browser? For example in the Document Browser if you click on "Spread" N4 spreads the *selection of text* (the highlighted area) to a larger segment, which can then be coded. In the Node Browser the same option spreads *the coding* to a wider selection of text, and instantly displays the results of the "spread" on screen.

10.1 Spreading & unspreading a text selection

We have been reflecting on what Jack has been talking about—he has described becoming less able to maintain his garden and house. We want to explore this phenomena further. We will now browse text and use Spread to extend the text selected to different segments of texts.

Step 1: Select the document you wish to browse, click on Browse.

Step 2: Select a segment of text by clicking and dragging down over the text.

Step 3: Click Spread or press "S".

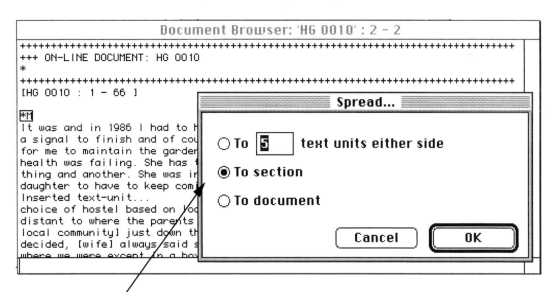

Click on the spread option you want. We have selected To section. For the option "text units either side" you need to nominate how many text units

Step 4: N4 opens up a dialogue box in which you can specify how you wish to spread the selection—to a number of text units either side of the selection, to the section or to the whole document. In this example we will spread to the section (revisit subheaders and creating sections on page 29). Then click OK.

The text unit range selected is extended to the section

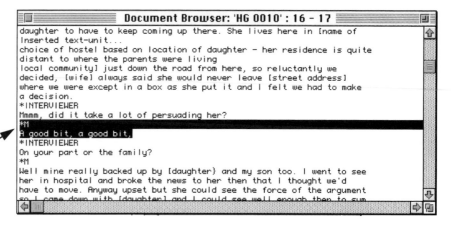

```
Document Browser: 'HG 0010' : 16 - 17
daughter to have to keep coming up there. She lives here in [name of
Inserted text-unit...
choice of hostel based on location of daughter - her residence is quite
distant to where the parents were living
local community] just down the road from here, so reluctantly we
decided, [wife] always said she would never leave [street address]
where we were except in a box as she put it and I felt we had to make
a decision.
*INTERVIEWER
Mmmm, did it take a lot of persuading her?
*M
A good bit, a good bit,
*INTERVIEWER
On your part or the family?
*M
Well mine really backed up by [daughter} and my son too. I went to see
her in hospital and broke the news to her then that I thought we'd
have to move. Anyway upset but she could see the force of the argument
so I came down with [daughter] and I could see well enough then to sum
```

Now, you can if you wish, code the selected text at a category by clicking on Add Indexing, and then select the codes at which you wish to code the text (revisit section 8.1 "Browsing and coding text on screen" on page 66.)

Step 5: If you find you don't want the selection spread in that way, click on Unspread and only the text units that were highlighted before you spread, will be highlighted.

You can also continue to spread (and unspread) the context to larger sections of text until you have enough text to code at a category. Or, through browsing the text, your question about it has been answered—you may not wish to code the text at any category!).

10.2 Spreading & unspreading coding

Let's now play with Spread and unspread in the Node Explorer. The line of text where Jack talks about being unable to maintain his garden has already been coded at a free node "hard to maintain" the fist time it was encountered. Other people have also talked about a similar experience during their interviews. Let's now go back to it and check it out some more.

the node "hard to maintain"

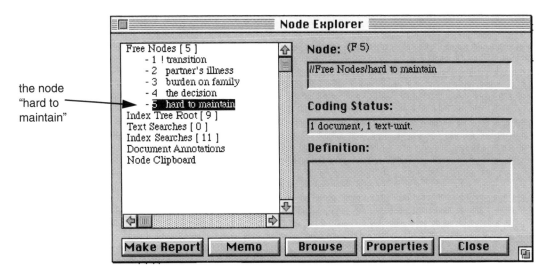

Step 1: In the Node Explorer, click on the node you wish to explore, then click Browse.

N4 opens up the Node Browser and you can review the text coded at the category "hard to maintain".

The text coded at "hard to maintain"

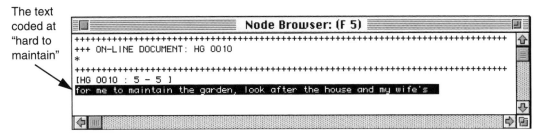

Step 2: To see more of the text surrounding that which is coded at a category, select a passage of text, and then click Spread.

Step 3: Choose a spread option in the dialogue box and click OK.

Spreading in the Node Browser, spreads the *coding* at this category to the bigger segment of text nominated in the Spread dialogue box. The Browser instantly displays the text *now* coded at that category.

Coding at "hard to maintain" has been spread to 2 units either side of the selection. All of these text units are now coded at this category.

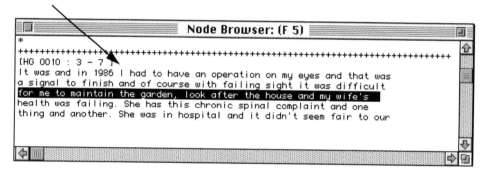

You may not want to keep that wider context coded here (for example you might have spread to section to see what issues or concerns led up to the passage of text being examined). If you do not want to keep the result of the spread you must click Unspread to remove the coding from the larger segment of text. If you want a larger segment, Spread again, and so on.

10.3 Browsing and jumping to the source document

Viewing a segment of text that is coded at a category can lead you to wonder about the source of the text—and its surrounding context. N4 provides you with the facility to jump from the Node Browser, to the Document Browser and the source of the text.

Step 1: In the Node Browser click on the text whose source you wish to view, then click Jump to source or press "J". N4 goes to the source document and opens it in the Document Browser.

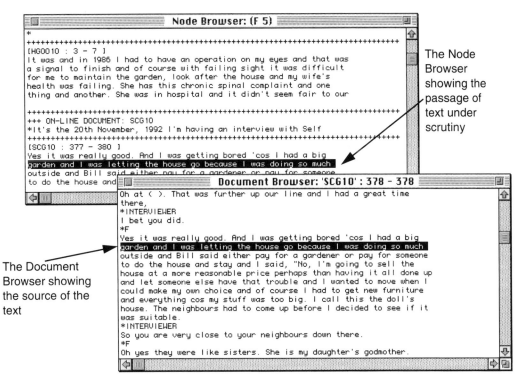

The Node Browser showing the passage of text under scrutiny

The Document Browser showing the source of the text

You are able to toggle or move between the two Browsers by clicking on the window you want to operate in. This provides you with the ability to continue browsing nodes, Jump to the source of text, and then moving back to the Node Browser to continue to browse text coded at a category.

10.4 Browsing and examining coding

We have browsed different segments of text and as well text coded at a category. If you wish, you can also examine *all* the coding of text in both the Document and Node Browsers. Through examining the coding you are able to view all the nodes at which a segment of text has been coded at, rather than examining the text unit references stored at a specific category.

Let's begin with the Node Explorer and all the text that has been coded at the category "hard to maintain" so far.

Step 1: Click on the node you want to browse, then click Browse. N4 opens up the familiar Node Browser display.

Step 2: Select the passage of text you wish to examine for coding, then click on eXamine coding or press "X".

N4 opens up a display which shows you *all* the nodes coding the text selected.

The passage of text in the
Node Explorer that is being
eXamined for coding

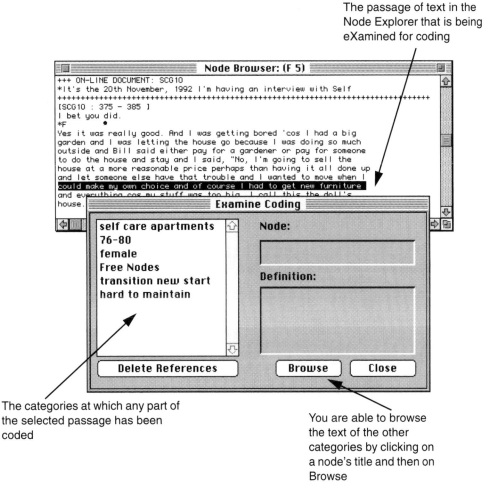

```
▦▬▬▬▬▬▬▬▬▬▬ Node Browser: (F 5) ▬▬▬▬▬▬▬▬▬▬ ▥
+++ ON-LINE DOCUMENT: SCG10                                              ⇧
*It's the 20th November, 1992 I'm having an interview with Self
++++++++++++++++++++++++++++++++++++++++++++++++++++++++++++++++++++++++++++
[SCG10 : 375 - 385 ]
I bet you did.
*F         •
Yes it was really good. And I was getting bored 'cos I had a big
garden and I was letting the house go because I was doing so much
outside and Bill said either pay for a gardener or pay for someone
to do the house and stay and I said, "No, I'm going to sell the
house at a more reasonable price perhaps than having it all done up
and let someone else have that trouble and I wanted to move when I
could make my own choice and of course I had to get new furniture
and everything cos my stuff was too big. I call this the doll's
house.                                                                   ⇩
◄▦▬▬▬▬▬▬▬▬▬▬▬▬ Examine Coding ▬▬▬▬▬▬▬▬▬▬▬▬▬ ►▨
```

```
┌──────────────────────────┐   Node:
│ self care apartments  ⇧ │   ┌──────────────────────┐
│ 76-80                   │   │                      │
│ female                  │   │                      │
│ Free Nodes              │   └──────────────────────┘
│ transition new start    │   Definition:
│ hard to maintain        │   ┌──────────────────────┐
│                         │   │                      │
│                         │   │                      │
│                       ⇩ │   └──────────────────────┘
└──────────────────────────┘
┌──────────────────────────┐   ┌──────────┐  ┌──────────┐
│  Delete References       │   │  Browse  │  │  Close   │
└──────────────────────────┘   └──────────┘  └──────────┘
```

The categories at which any part of
the selected passage has been
coded

You are able to browse
the text of the other
categories by clicking on
a node's title and then on
Browse

Step 3: If you wish, you can browse the text coded at the
other categories by clicking on a node's title, then the
button Browse inside this dialogue box.

In this way you are able to move inside the Node Explorer and browse first the text of one category than another.

By combining process such as Jump to source you can move from the Node Explorer to the source of a text segment, and then examine coding of text in the Document Browser.

10.5 Browsing and removing coding at a node

During your exploration of coding you may find text has been coded at a category that you no longer want coded there You can remove it from a category as you come across it.

In the Examine Coding dialogue box there is a button "Delete References. By clicking on a node title, and then clicking Delete References, N4 deletes the coding for that node.

The Delete References button deletes coding at the selected node

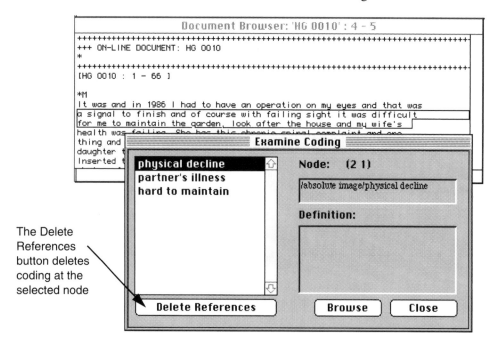

Alternatively you can use the option Remove in the palette.

Step 1: Click on the node in the Node Explorer you wish to browse, then click Browse.

Step 2: Click on the text that you no longer wish coded at that category, then click Remove or press "R".

Step 3: N4 queries you to make sure of your action. If you are, then click Yes.

The selected text unit is instantaneously removed from the Node Browser and is no longer coded at that category.

All these processes provide ways for you to examine coding and data in different context, and to continue to review and revise the way in which you are structuring data through your index system. Moving interactively between the Browsers creates a closeness to data and to categories as you continue to shuffle, refine, review and reorganise—until the dance is completed.

The next chapter explores text searches as another way of exploring and coding data. We also look at the tools provided in N4 to craft the results of text searches.

11

SEARCHING TEXT

We have talked about qualitative data as being voluminous, unstructured, rich and textual. Text is made up of words, sentences, phrases—all parts of speech. This characteristic of textual data can be utilized in analysis to explore and organize concepts by using N4's ability to search text and to store the results as a node.

In N4 you able to search for strings *and* patterns of characters. This section explores this tool and presents some practical examples of how it may be utilized in a project to explore and organize concepts, and to aid specific coding tasks.

11.1 Why do text searches?

Text searches have a role in finding and collecting together all occurrences of a word or a phase (or whatever you wish to specify!) which is meaningful to your analysis. In these searches, the words people use to describe their experience, are utilized to describe and name phenomena or locate phenomena in the text.

Using a text search provides a way to *quickly* pull together all material containing a reference to a word, or group of words or patterns of characters. If this process was undertaken using a line by line, or even paragraph by paragraph approach, it would take much longer. What is important to remember is that a text search does not distinguish *context*—that is your job as the researcher. N4 provides tools which help pull together potentially relevant text, and eliminates text you don't want from a search.

Text searches also play an important role in aiding some repetitive coding tasks. This is particularly relevant in specific research projects where data (or part of the data) has a recurring structure which is important in its analysis. For instance questions in a structured survey; speakers in an interview or group discussion; or a known set of demographic attributes for each participant. In these instances the "structure" is utilized in a text search to gather together the bits you want to code at a category for the whole project.

The String Text Search dialogue box is presented below and shows the options available to you in Text Searches.

The type of search you are currently conducting—a string search

Type the string of characters you wish to search for in here

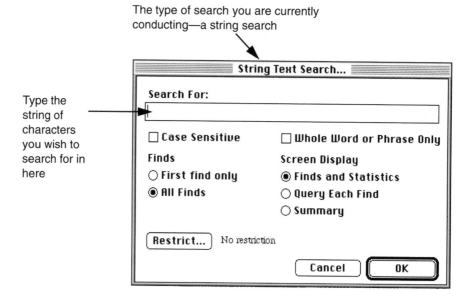

11.2 What is a string search?

A string search finds every text unit which contains an exact or literal match to the sequence of characters typed into the Search Text dialogue box. A 'character' may be letters, digits, punctuation and other non–alphabetical characters, such as brackets, hyphens, or spaces. A string search is usually a word or a phrase.

In our project *Getting On* a word such as "old" could be used to find text where respondents refer to themselves or their peers as being "old". If no restrictions are placed on this search it could find "old", "olden", "older", and also "hold". Some of these finds may be relevant to the concept we are exploring, but others will simply yield unrelated material.

A text search without any restrictions is like a very large, non–selective net that pulls in the fish, the dolphins, the beer can and floating wrecks!

The options provided in the search dialogue box help to distinguish between the text that is meaningful and what simply gets caught along the way, by providing ways in which bits can be eliminated and not saved as part of the find.

11.3 What is a pattern search?

Pattern searches allow you to search for *patterns* or combinations of characters rather than an exact match to specified characters. To create pattern searches a number of special characters are used to specify what combination of characters you want to search for. In this way pattern searches allow you, for instance, to search for words with similar meanings or usage in dialogue, or words with a common stem or beginning. The full range of special characters is described in the *User's Guide* and also in the Help system in N4.

Two frequently used pattern searches can locate clusters of words or different forms of a word.

Finding words with common meanings

In our project *Getting On* we could search for words which indicate that a participant may have experience some type of fall. A search for occurrences of words such as "fell", "slipped" or "tripped" might be useful.

The expression (or what you type into the Search Text Dialogue box) begins and closes with square brackets "[ ]" and each word is separated with a straight bar "(|")" with no spaces between any of the characters. My pattern search would look like:

$$[fell|slipped|tripped]$$

N4 searches for "fell" or "slipped" or "tripped". If it finds an occurrence of any of these words in a text unit, it reports it as a find, and moves onto the next text unit.

Find different forms of words

This search locates a word and its possible endings. In this search the stem or common beginning of the word is typed followed by a square bracket, inside which are the different endings of the word each separated by the vertical bar. The expression to find "trip", "tripping" or "tripped" looks like this:

$$trip[ped|ping]$$

11.4 What does N4 search?

N4 searches the text of imported documents. During the search, it searches all parts of a document's text—*except for the header*—text unit by text unit. If a find is made in a text unit, N4 will stop searching the rest of the text unit and start searching the next one.

Because N4 uses a text unit as the basic unit to which it refers to, it reports *counts of text units* in which occurrences of the specified characters were found, rather than how many times the characters actually occurred. If a group of characters occurs more than once in a text unit it is reported only once.

11.5   What happens to the finds?

All finds are saved as *a node* which is placed in the Text Search area. Now that we have the results of the search for "fall", it is necessary to make a number of decisions about what to do with the results—Is the result meaningful to my analysis? And if so, in what way? Do I wish to keep the results? If so, where in the index system is the best place to put the node?

The node created through the search, like any other node can be browsed; spread; merged into an existing node; attached to the index tree as a new node; placed in the Free Nodes area; left in the Text Search area (and renamed!) or deleted from the project.

Spreading the results of a find

A text search will collect references to just the text units in which a find was made. You may wish to include text around a find to provide context to the specific piece of text you found. This is particularly relevant where smaller text units, for instance a line, have been adopted for a project. Spreading a find can be used in specific situations: where a find for a specific question which was entered as a subheader, can be spread to the section to include the responses to the question; or where a find of all respondents with a specific demographic attribute (such as type of living environment) is spread to the whole document. (Revisit "Spreading & unspreading a text selection" on page 91.)

Merging the "new" node into an old node

A text search may have yielded data which is relevant to a node that is already part of the index stem. If this is that case the node can be merged into an existing node. Its text references are simple added to those already stored at that node. (Revisit "Combining categories" on page 83.)

Attaching the "new" node to the index system

A search may have yielded material which represents a new category in the project. This category may be added to the index system as a new node by placing it in the Index Tree or Free Nodes. (Revisit "Shifting a node or subtree to a different place" on page 80.)

11.6 Doing a text search

Whether you are conducting a string or pattern search there are a number of options which are provided in the dialogue box which are useful in specific context. Using a string search we will work through doing a text search, the options available, and how these options relate to the specific needs of particular problems in research projects.

In our project *Getting On* the transcriptions of interview have been set up so that subheaders indicate a change in speaker. The interview schedule used in the project was unstructured and followed very broad theme areas. Coding all the interviewer's dialogue at a category will provide a way to review the theme areas covered in each interview. We are then able to look for similarities and differences in topics or issues covered in all interviews. We also want to know what the respondents said! To do this we will code each speaker's dialogue at three nodes: interviewer, male respondent and female respondent. Later we will use these nodes to restrict searches to text coded at them.

To begin, we will do a Text Search to find the subheader *INTERVIEWER, which we will spread to the section, and then merge the resultant node into the node "interviewer" in the Index Tree.

Step 1: From the menu choose Documents, Search Text and choose String Search. The dialogue box is opened and you can type in the string or pattern you wish to search for.

Step 2: Type in "*INTERVIEWER" and click OK.

A string search is a literal match to the specified characters. If you typed a space after the "*" in any document the search will not find this version of the string of characters.

The string we are
searching for

Making a search
"Case Sensitive" and/
or "Whole Word or
Phrase Only" makes
the search more
restrictive and less
likely to yield
irrelevant material

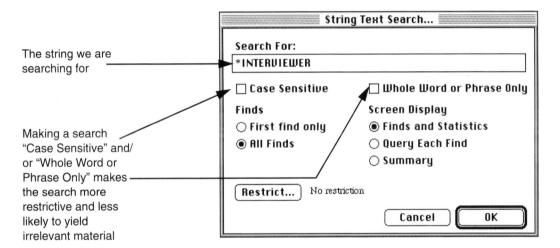

N4 searches all the documents in the project and stores all finds as a new node—(T 1). If we browsed the node we would find only the subheaders "*INTERVIEWER" stored at this node.

Text Search Report showing the
results of the search

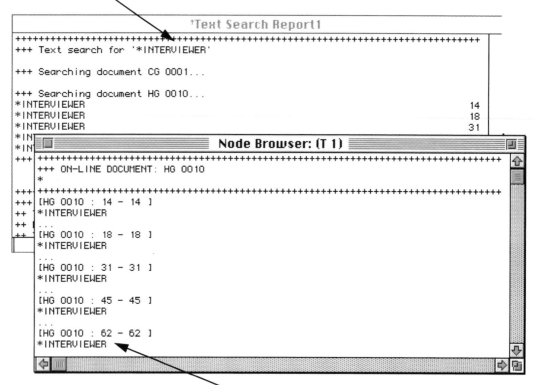

Browsing the new node shows that only the
subheaders are coded at the new node (T 1)

We also want the text following the subheader—what
the interviewer said—coded at this node. To do this
(instead of paragraph by paragraph for all documents
in this project!) we simply spread the node to the section and the interviewer's dialogue will be coded at
the node (T 1).

Step 3: Select (T 1) in the Node Explorer and call up the Node pop–up menu and choose Spread.

Click on the node you wish to spread

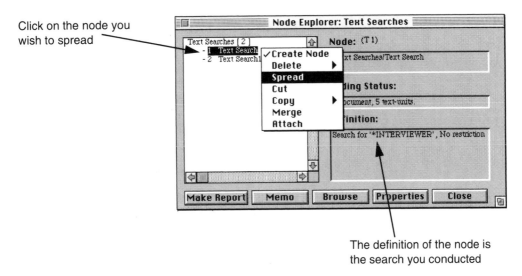

Node Explorer: Text Searches

Text Searches [2]
- 1 Text Search
- 2 Text Search1

✓ Create Node
Delete ▶
Spread
Cut
Copy ▶
Merge
Attach

Node: (T 1)

xt Searches/Text Search

ding Status:
ocument, 5 text-units.

inition:
Search for '*INTERVIEWER', No restriction

Make Report | Memo | Browse | Properties | Close

The definition of the node is the search you conducted

Step 4: Click on the radio button To section and click OK.

The interviewer's dialogue is coded at (T 1) and immediately displayed in the Node Browser.

Node Browser: (T 1)

```
++++++++++++++++++++++++++++++++++++++++++++++++++++++++++++++++++++++++++++++
+++ ON-LINE DOCUMENT: HG 0010
*
++++++++++++++++++++++++++++++++++++++++++++++++++++++++++++++++++++++++++++++
[HG 0010 : 14 - 15 ]
*INTERVIEWER
Mmmm, did it take a lot of persuading her?
...
[HG 0010 : 18 - 19 ]
*INTERVIEWER
On your part or the family?
...
[HG 0010 : 31 - 33 ]
*INTERVIEWER
And how did you get on with disposing of your house? Did your children
have a role in that. Did the family keep the house or...
...
[HG 0010 : 45 - 47 ]
*INTERVIEWER
```

The subheader *INTERVIEWER and the section (what the interviewer said) is now coded at (T 1)

11.6.1 Do you want the search to be Case sensitive?

Making a search case sensitive tells N4 to match the *case* of the characters as well. So, if you type "*interviewer" (with a lower case) and then click the case sensitive box, N4 will find *interviewer" but not "*INTERVIEWER". (In our project it would find nothing!)

Case sensitive searchers are useful if you are searching for particular instances of things such as proper nouns or where you have used particular capitalization of words or phrases to mark text in some way. (You may have used capitalisation to indicate your own commentary inserted into the flow of text.)

11.6.2 Do you want the search to find whole word or phrase only?

If you need to restrict the search to find only the exact matches for the word or phrase you typed into the search dialogue, make sure you check "Whole word or phrase only". In our project not many men report experiencing a fall or are reported to have fallen. The search for "he fell", with the option whole word or phrase only selected, will only find "he fell" but not "she fell".

11.6.3 What documents do you want to search?

Here you are able to search all the documents in the project or restrict the search to include or exclude documents coded at a specified node. In this way the search can be restricted to a sub-group of documents or cases.

In *Getting On* we have interviews with people from three different residential environments. We have in our Index Tree a sub-tree which has a node for each environment. We have used these nodes to record a respondent's living environment. We want to compare the differences between these environments, so in our search we can include *just* the documents for "hostel" respondents. Or we could *exclude* all the documents for "own home" respondents, and search documents for "hostel" and "self–care apartments". How do the results compare? Are there differences between the groups and how they describe feeling happy?

Restricting a Text Search to include or exclude groups of documents is like using a node as a filter through which the results of a search are viewed. These results, if you wish, can be saved as a new node.

11.6.4	**What screen display do you want to interact with during the search?**

There are three options you can choose from which require varying degrees of interaction between you and the search process.

Finds and statistics

A screen at the end of the search process provides a log of:

- what word, phrase or pattern was searched for;

- which documents were searched;

- the text unit or text unit range in which finds were located; and,

- descriptive statistics about the Text Search.

Query each find

This option allows you to choose whether a find is saved as part of the result. This function is useful to eliminate finds that are inappropriate or you don't want. For example a find for "fall" can describe a person falling or a person's observation of what happens to leaves in autumn in their garden! By querying each find you are able to select only the first instance of the occurrence and reject all others. Only text passages which include "fall" *in the context* you are exploring are saved as a node.

A summary

A summary is very fast and useful if you are want everything to be saved as part of the find. In our example we would choose this option because we want to keep every find for "*INTER-VIEWER".

11.6.5 What finds do you want?

All finds

All finds retrieves every text unit in which there is a find.

First find only

First find only retrieves only the first occurrence in a document and will then skip over the rest of the document and start searching the next document. This is useful if you are using a text search to locate key words or phrases. In the project *Getting On* information for each respondent was typed at the beginning of an interview and included information on group membership, age and so on. When searching for these attributes, N4 can be asked to looked for each attribute at the beginning of the document only, and then skipped over the rest of the text to the next document.

Text Searches are a way in which the intrinsic strength of qualitative data—words and phrases—can be used to explore data and to integrate the results of searches into your project as nodes. They play an important role in quickly gathering together material across the project, which you can then make decisions about—Is this meaningful? If so, how can it be integrating into my index system? Text Searches are one way to ask questions and save the answers to these questions as nodes. The next chapter explores another way—the Index Searches.

12

SEARCHING THE INDEX SYSTEM

The overall analysis process is a search for understanding so that you are able to explain the thing you are exploring—to yourself and a wider community or audience. In many ways it is rendering an account —your account—of a situation, and event or process through telling a story or narrative.

In our project *Getting On* we are moving into exploring and understanding the many meanings of the node "absolute image of old age" and how this concept relates to others. What might we want to ask next…? What tools would we need?

While many researchers are interested in each category and what is held within it, others are also interested in exploring and testing the interrelationships between groups of categories in the index system. In N4 relationships and categories can be chased by asking questions about the coding using a range of Index Searches.

The Index Searches offer ways of seeking, validating and illuminating phenomena, and the emerging story about the data, by exploring codes and coding and how they have been used. Several searches are designed to pull out different aspects of the relationships which may exists between codes.

If codes are used inconsistently across documents; if meaning associated with codes shifts throughout analysis without a purposeful redefinition of the category; or if coding is patchy—all of these things will be reflected in the outcome of the Index Search. In the same way, if you are not clear about what relationship you are trying to explore in the data, the selection of "which search?" becomes problematic and the results remain conceptually perplexing rather than illuminating.

And when we have asked those questions, what would we want to do with the answer? Ask another question? "*Who* has this image? We could build on the answer. So, the outcome or result of an Index Search is itself a new node or category which is placed in the index system as a node.

These nodes—like every other node in the index system—hold coding and may be browsed. In this way, Index Searches contribute to the development of new categories and coding, and may themselves be used in a further search.

Question and answer are part of an iterative cycle, with each new question creating a new view of the data, which can in turn be integrated into the index system, and become part of the next question.

The Node Explorer showing nodes created through an Index Search

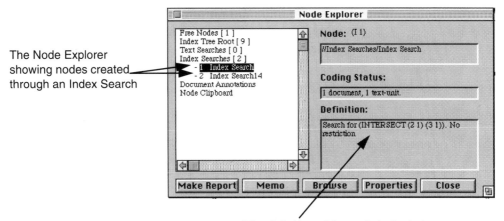

The definition of the node is the Index Search that was conducted

The Index system can undergo rapid and radical change during Index Searches. Some researchers experience this phase in a project as de–stabilizing. Many new nodes can be created relatively quickly demanding decisions to be made their placement in the index system—if at all! In many ways it is through this process of "de–stabilization" or "renewed fluidity" that the index system regenerates itself and moves to a new period of stability and cohesion. Without this phase, relationships between categories would remain relatively unexplored and analysis would stop at examining each node or category as an entity.

12.1 The Index Searchers

There are four groups of Index Searches, with seventeen searches in total. The schema below shows an overview of the operators and their subgroupings. Each group of operators is different in function.

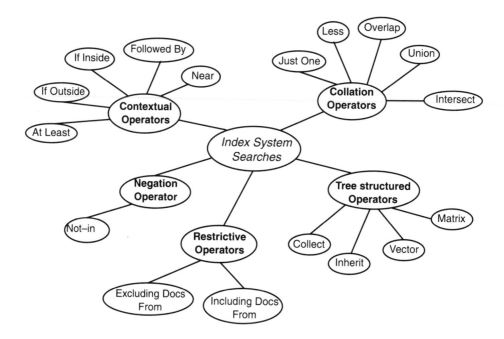

The next chapter describes what each does, and why you would reach for that particular tool. But first, here are the simple steps you take to request and specify an Index Search.

12.1.1 Selecting which operator

Each operator explores a specific relationship between nodes. Which operator to choose depends on the nature of the relationship between nodes that you wish to explore. Each operator is selected through the IndexSystem menu.

Step 1: Go to the menu IndexSystem, and choose Index Search. A submenu lists all the operators.

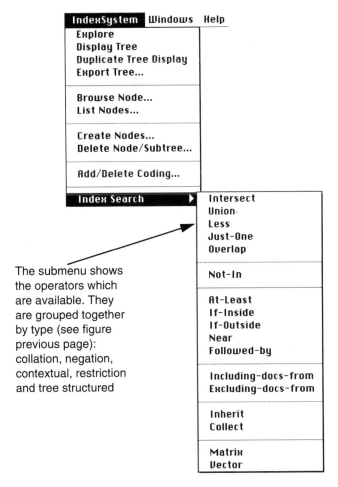

The submenu shows the operators which are available. They are grouped together by type (see figure previous page): collation, negation, contextual, restriction and tree structured

Step 2: Choose the search you wish to conduct and N4 opens up a Index Search dialogue box.

In the Index Search dialogue box there are a number of options which allow you to place restrictions on a search, define a context and specify what references from the search to retrieve. As we work through each of the Index Searches in the next chapter (see page 123) we will explore these options. Then, in Chapter 14 (see page 139) we will look at ways in which the result of searches can be displayed and reported to support analysis and writing.

12.1.2 Nominating which nodes

For all the operators you will need to nominate which nodes to include in the search. You may type in the node addresses or select them through the Select button. To enter more than one node address, type them in parentheses and separate them with a comma.

The screen below is the dialogue box for an Intersect search. The nodes (2 1) and (F 4) have been typed into the search window.

Node addresses have been typed in. Each address is enclosed in parentheses with a comma separating each address

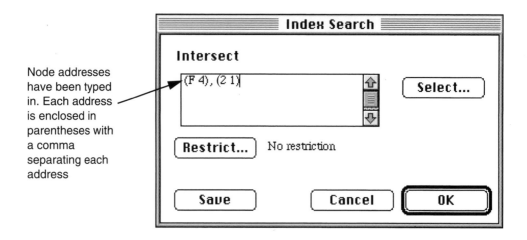

12.1.3 Defining the context

A context will need to be defined for some searches. There are three "contexts" which are available to you (as there are for Spread)—text units, section and document.

We want to explore how people talk about making a decision to move to a retirement village *Near* where they may have talked about no longer coping with their garden. In this search we will specify near as being within 5 text units.

What context you choose is dependent on how closely together you would like the coding to be and your text unit size. Specifying five lines is very different to specifying five paragraphs.

Step 1: Click on the radio button for the context you wish to select.

Step 2: If you chose Text Units it is necessary to nominate how many by typing a number. The screen shows 5 text units have been specified for this search.

5 text units have been specified

Click on a radio button to make your selection

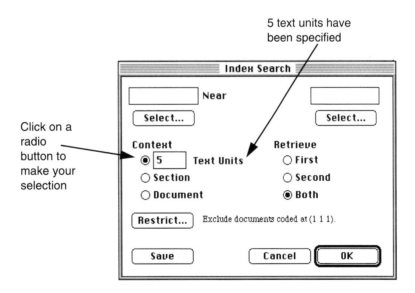

12.1.4 Defining a restriction for a search

The Restriction option enables you to specify which documents or which text is searched based on its coding. The ability to pin-point the search provides you with the tools to unravel and tease out delicately the relationships being explored. The ability to restrict to either specific documents or to specific text enables you to subset the data in multiple ways, thus providing strong support for processes such as case analysis.

We might now want to explore whether having a spouse with a chronic disease also affected the decision to move to a retirement village. So, we can restrict the search to only documents coded at node "spouse with chronic illness". Or we could examine cases where the element of chronic illness is absent, by excluding text or documents coded at this node from the search.

Step 1: Click on the Restrict button.

N4 opens up the Restriction dialogue box.

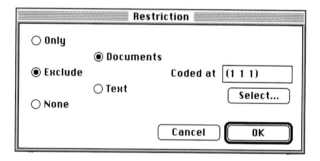

Step 2: Click on the radio button Only or Exclude or None to specify *how* you wish to restrict the search.

Step 3: Then click on Document or Text to specify to *what* you want the restriction to apply.

Step 4: Type in or use the Select button to nominate which node address you wish to use, and click OK.

The restriction that you have set will then be shown in the Index Search dialogue box.

Restriction that is currently specified is shown. Only documents coded at (3 1) will be included in the Index Search

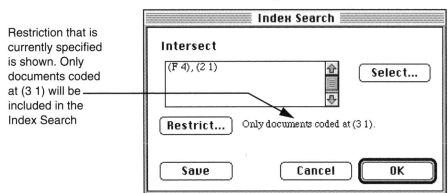

12.1.5 Defining the retrieval

For two searches you will be asked to select which references you would like N4 to retrieve. The options available to you are:

- the first node's references

- the second node's references, or

- both sets of references.

Click on a radio button to specify which references you want to retrieve from the search

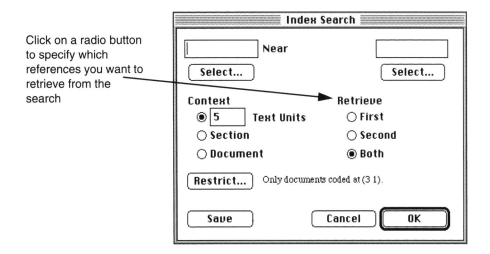

In the next chapter, we'll do 'real' searches to ask real questions and show you how you can think more about the results, ask further questions and build up your theory!

13

ASKING QUESTIONS ABOUT CODING

We have talked about the way searching the index system can become an iterative cycle of asking questions and seeking answers to those questions. Each phase of questioning creating a new view of the data, which in turn becomes part of the next phase of questioning.

It is this process of weaving multiple views of data, which is the next phase of analysis, as we use the Index Searches to build up our theory out of the data.

This chapter presents seventeen questions which we could ask in our project *Getting On*. These questions represent N4's seventeen Index Searches. These questions are a tiny handful of what could be asked. They are meant to shed light on how you go about asking questions of codes and coding and are illustrative only. What is important to remember throughout, is that for every question we have asked, there are many more to be asked! Just like there are more document to be imported, more nodes to be created and coded at, and much more development the index system will undergo before the project reaches cohesion and stability.

For now, lets examine some of the questions we can ask, and the searches we can use in each of these context.

The Index Searches are organised in five groups.

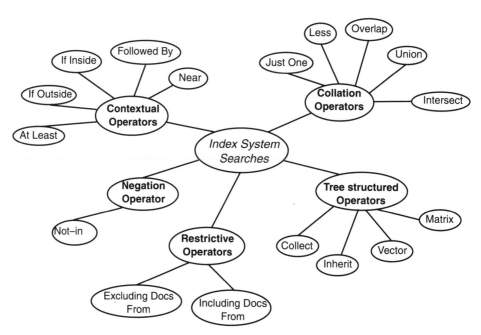

Each search creates a new node and places it into the Index Search area of the index system. As you work through the searches take time to browse the results and use some of the tools presented in Chapter 9 "Crafting the index system" on page 79 and Chapter 10 "Interactive Browsing" on page 89. Play with the results and use them to extend your thinking about your data—and your analysis!

13.1 The collation operators

The collation operators pull together text coded at categories within specified relationships. Each search involves two or more nodes. These searches can be further restricted by including or excluding in the search, documents or text coded at a node.

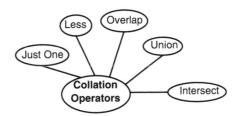

The dialogue box for all of the collation operators is identical. and its structure is illustrated below.

Type of search

The nodes included in the search

The restriction applied to the search

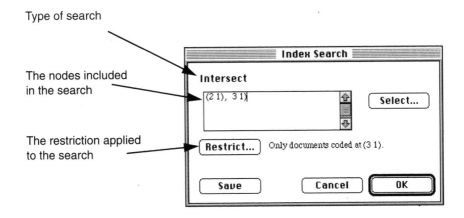

Intersect

Where people talk about experiencing physical decline do they also talk about finding their domestic environments hard to maintain?

We will search for the intersect of "hard to maintain" and "physical decline". An Intersect finds all text which is coded by all of the nominated nodes.

A diagrammatic representation of the result is shown below.

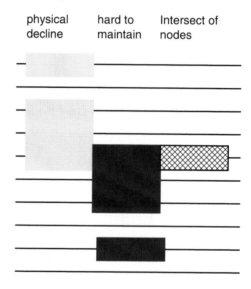

Interesting? We might be intrigued that coding at these two concepts is not more linked. *"Are there differences between people who live independently in the community and those in the self care apartments and how they talk about these two things?"*

We will further restrict the search and include only documents coded at "self care apartments" in our intersect, and so on. Each result is built on until we have exhausted this line of inquiry.

Union

We have coded for both chronic illness and frailty. I wonder how different these two concepts really are?

Union finds all text units which are coded at any of the nominated nodes. Union is a good way of collecting together material to view it as a whole, or to pull together concepts which appear to be the same, and to explore how similar or dissimilar they may be. A union can also be used to merge more than two nodes in a single operation.

Overlap

Now that we have viewed all text for chronic illness and frailty, we want to continue teasing these concepts apart. There appears to be similarity between these two concepts, but where in the text do these concepts overlap each other?

Overlap finds all text units which are coded by two nominated nodes if their text unit *range*s overlap. This means that the two segments of text coded at the nodes have in common at least one text unit. It is a union where there is an intersection.

Less

There are a number of people who have talked about the transition between living independently in the community and moving into a retirement village. Many of our early ideas were about this critical time of transition. Do some people found this period a positive and rich experience rather than a difficult and anguished time?

We will use the Less operator to locate passages of text where people talk about transition, but in the absence of dialogue in the same text passages, where they speak of transition as a difficult period. Less finds all text units which are coded at the first node but not the second node.

Just–one

We want to extend this exploration further. Do people talk about transition in just rich and positive terms or in anguished and difficult ones? Is transition a blend of these experiences?

Just one finds those text units which are coded by only one of the specified nodes.

13.2 Contextual operators

Contextual searches involve asking questions about how text is coded by a node in context of coding by another node. These searches find codes which show relationships such as proximity or sequencing of coding.

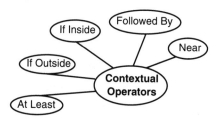

Near

We want to explore how people talk about making a decision to move to a retirement village, and where, close by, they talk about experiencing diminishing physical capacity. Are these two concepts associated together?

The operator Near defines proximity—and you get to choose how close—by defining a context for the retrieval. In analysis this enables you to explore how dialogue about a concept is located near dialogue about another concept.

Followed–by

These two things—moving and experiencing diminishing physical capacity do seem to be associated? Do people talk about a sense of losing physical capacity and then talk about making a decision to move? Or do people, during reflection, present the sense of losing physical capacity as part of what was happening generally—now that they have moved, there is a realisation about how much not coping physically impacted everyday life and their sense of personal well–being?

Followed–by defines sequence of concepts in text. Does the move follow the realization?

At–least

The move and what triggers it? There seem to be multiple elements. Can just one element be a trigger? Or is it a cluster of things like: a storm wrecking the garden, falling over in the shower, feeling lonely, losing a spouse, the children putting pressure on, not wanting to be a burden to the family, a sense of fairness to the family?

At–least will search for clusters of coding within the context of a section or a document. This operator will find all text units coded by the named nodes if the minimum number of nodes have references in a section or document.

Type in here the minimum number of nodes that must occur in the section or document. This number must be less than the total number of node addresses typed into the search window

Type in here the node addresses of the cluster that you are searching for

Context defines that the cluster of nodes must occur in a section or document.
Click on the radio button to select which context

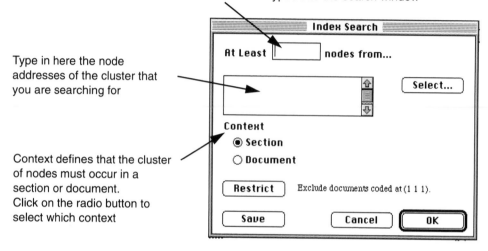

If–inside

Let's continue to explore the clustering of things which trigger a move? Let's explore our new node "the things that trigger" and find out if people talk about these things inside text passages where they also talk about becoming a resident of a retirement village?

If–inside is an operator involving two categories. This search will find all text units for a node if its text unit range *is enclosed by* the text unit range of another node.

If–outside

Or does it happen the other way round? Is moving not the focus we thought it was? Are "the things that trigger" a bigger conversation inside which there is a smaller conversation about moving?

If–outside is the flipside of If–inside This operator will find all text units of a category *if its text unit encloses* the text unit range of another category.

13.3 The negation operator

Do people in self–care apartments not talk about the transition?

There is only one negation operator—Not In. This operator searches for data not indexed at a node. It can be further restricted to documents or text coded at a nominated node.

```
╔══════════════════ Index Search ══════════════════╗
║                                                   ║
║   Not In      ┌──────────────┐   ┌───────────┐    ║
║               │              │   │  Select...│    ║
║               └──────────────┘   └───────────┘    ║
║                                                   ║
║   ┌───────────┐  Exclude documents coded at (1 1 1). ║
║   │ Restrict..│                                   ║
║   └───────────┘                                   ║
║                                                   ║
║   ┌───────────┐      ┌──────────┐ ┌──────────┐    ║
║   │   Save    │      │  Cancel  │ │    OK    │    ║
║   └───────────┘      └──────────┘ └──────────┘    ║
╚═══════════════════════════════════════════════════╝
```

13.4 Restrictive operators

Restrictive Operators search data coded *by a node* but restricts or limits the search to a subset of documents.These operators are very useful for splitting data coded for a category into groups. This operator can be further defined by a restriction, thus allowing high degrees of specificity in the questions that you're able to ask of the data.

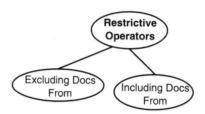

The dialogue box for both of these operators is identical.

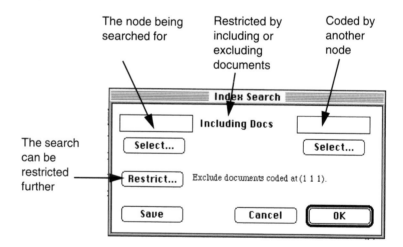

Including–docs–from

We have been reflecting on the category "loss of identity". How is this sense of loss expressed by people in the hostel group?

This search will find text unit references for a category but restricts the search to only those documents which are coded by another category.

In our exploration of how a loss of identity is expressed in dialogue, we are able to split the data into subgroups such as living environment, so that questions about coding can be asked in context of attributes shared by subgroups. We can then explore how these concepts are expressed by each subgroup, if we wish. Are there any differences? What other questions do we need to ask of the coding to explore how these subgroups may be the same—or different?

Excluding–docs–from

Do people in the self care apartments and those living independently in the community share expressions of loss? Or are expressions shared by those in the hostel and self–care apartments?

This search will find text unit references for a category but restricts the search by excluding those documents which are coded by another category.

13.5 Tree structured operators

The Tree structured searchers utilise the hierarchical organization of the Index Tree. If you have a flat system these operators can not be utilized.

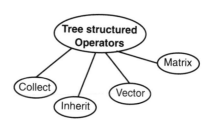

Collect

We want to re–examine the concept absolute image. What do all the text passages look like together? Do they all belong in this category or is there another way we can view (and code) this data?

A Collect is like a union, or doing multiple merges of nodes into one node. A Collect search merges together the node specified and all the nodes *below* it in the tree. This search is useful for bringing together material at a higher or more general level of abstraction, so that dimensions of categories can be seen together at their meta level.

Coding which is implicit at the more general level of the subtree is also made explicit and can be browsed and used in further searches as an entity.

A collect on the node "absolute image" will merge all six nodes within the boxed area of the diagram. A collect on the node "physical decline" will merge only the four nodes shown in the grey area.

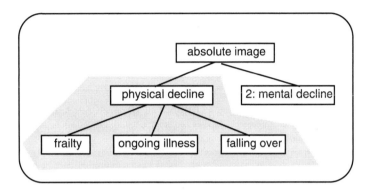

Inherit

Inherit searches for and merges its ancestor nodes—all those *above* itself in the tree. An Inherit search on the node "frailty" creates a new node which is the union of physical decline and absolute image. It does not merge itself into the new node.

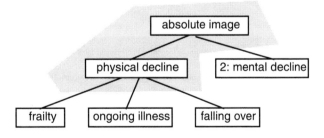

Matrix

We have spent a lot of time thinking about images of old age held by older people. While older people do appear to hold a view of "what it is like to be at the end of life" we want to tease apart further who holds this view. Do only people living in retirement villages hold this view? Is it shared by those living independently in the community? Are there differences in how each group express this concept?

A matrix is like doing a "cross tabulation" of data. N4 takes the children of the first node and cross tabulates them with the children of the second node, and creates a matrix of cells to show the result of the search. The new node is stored in the index system as a matrix node and is displayed in the tree as a stacked rectangle (rather than the single rectangle). Matrix nodes cannot have children, nor can they be used in a further search. A number of operators can be used to construct matrix nodes:

- Intersect

- Union

- Less

- Just–one

- Overlap

- If–inside

- If–outside

- Near

- Followed–by

Matrices play an important role in projects where related categories are being explored in relation to other related categories; for example how do participants from each of the residential settings portray the two domains of the category "absolute image".

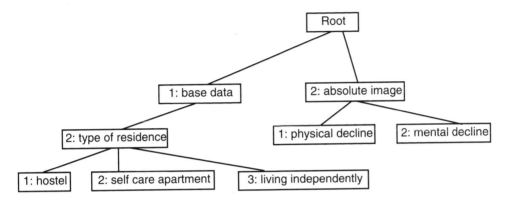

N4 reports each cell of the matrix and returns text unit references, if there are finds for that cell. To see the text in each cell, you make a report on the matrix node (revisit "Making a report of a category" on page 140). To see the numbers you export the table (see "Displaying tables" on page 146).

Vector

Let's compare how different age groups talk about the concept "absolute image" rather than its subcategories. Does age make a difference?

Let's use our new node—the one we created with a Collect on the node "absolute image" and use it in a Vector where we Intersect "age group" and "absolute image".

A vector is like a matrix but it is one row. A vector takes the address of the first node "absolute image" (not its children) and the children of the second node address "age group" and constructs one row of cells. The same list of operators can be used in Vectors as in a matrix.

The next chapter presents an exploration of data display, model-ling and reporting. While it is the finishing chapter of the book it is in no way the conclusion of our project. There are still many iterative loops to move through as analysis weaves it dance through the data. In many ways the final chapter is a way to commence the next loop!

14

SYNTHESIS

We have come a long way. We have created a new project, pre-pared documents, imported documents, and as well, added external documents. We have reflected on documents, recording our emerging ideas as they occurred to us, and coded and re–coded them. We have created an index system to reflect our thinking about our data and, as our thinking evolved, we re–organised it. We have also asked questions about patterns of coding using the index searches, and have integrated the results into the project as new thinking and new categorization.

N4 provides a range of tools for displaying data throughout analysis. This chapter presents an exploration of some of these tools provided in N4 to display the results of your analysis—the patterns of coding of a document; the outcomes of a search; the coding status of a category or document; or the results of coding at a category. These tools allow you to see the outcomes from your project and provide support to interpretation and writing. Many of these data displays can also be integrated directly into your writing.

14.1 Making a report of a category

We have already made a number of reports from N4 which we have used during other analysis processes (revisit "Coding off the computer, then entering coding later" on page 70). We will now make a report of a category so that we are able to view all text which has been coded at that category.

Step 1: Select the node you wish to report on in the Node Explorer.

Step 2: Click on the Make Report button. N4 opens up the Make Node Report dialogue box.

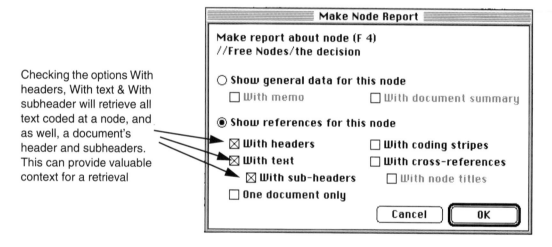

Checking the options With headers, With text & With subheader will retrieve all text coded at a node, and as well, a document's header and subheaders. This can provide valuable context for a retrieval

The dialogue box has two main sections: the first provides you with the option to show general data for the node which will retrieve the memo and/or a document summary. The document summary presents descriptive data for a node and its coding status. The summary includes the node definition (if it has one), when it was created and last modified, a list of its siblings and children (if it has any), each document it codes, and as well the percentage of documents in the project coded by it.

The second option in this dialogue box allows you to retrieve references for the nodes including the header, subheaders, text and coding.

This report has many uses including; viewing coding in a document or across all the material in the project, and showing patterns of coding for passages of text. It can indicate how pervasive or otherwise a category is in the project or a document.

We will retrieve for this node the text which is referenced to it, and as well, headers and subheaders.

Step 3: Click on the radio button Show references for this node, then click on each option that you wish to retrieve (the boxes should be marked with a cross).

Step 4: Click OK.

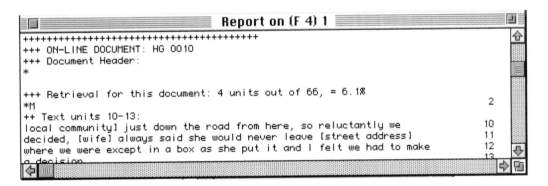

```
+++++++++++++++++++++++++++++++++++++++++++++
+++ ON-LINE DOCUMENT: HG 0010
+++ Document Header:
*

+++ Retrieval for this document: 4 units out of 66, = 6.1%
*M                                                                    2
++ Text units 10-13:
local community] just down the road from here, so reluctantly we      10
decided, [wife] always said she would never leave [street address]    11
where we were except in a box as she put it and I felt we had to make  12
a decision                                                            13
```

N4 opens up a report window. This report is a text file which is a copy of text held in the database. It can be edited, printed and saved. From this report you can, if you wish, copy and paste into your paper, extracts to illustrate and evidence your writing.

At the end of the report N4 gives descriptive percentages of the coding for this category.

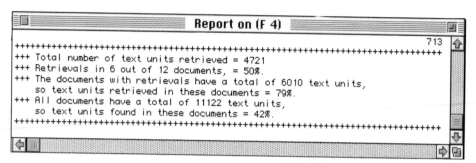

```
▓▓▓▓▓▓▓▓▓▓▓▓▓▓▓▓▓▓ Report on (F 4) ▓▓▓▓▓▓▓▓▓▓▓▓▓▓▓▓
                                                              713
+++++++++++++++++++++++++++++++++++++++++++++++++++++++++++++++++
+++ Total number of text units retrieved = 4721
+++ Retrievals in 6 out of 12 documents, = 50%.
+++ The documents with retrievals have a total of 6010 text units,
     so text units retrieved in these documents = 79%.
+++ All documents have a total of 11122 text units,
     so text units found in these documents = 42%.
+++++++++++++++++++++++++++++++++++++++++++++++++++++++++++++++++
```

This summary provides you with information on how many documents are coded at this category in the whole project, the density of coding in the documents where text is referenced to the node, and other information including numbers and percentages of text units which are referenced to it.

14.2 Making a report to display coding in a document

Reports which display coding have a variety of uses including showing you how coding of a document is progressing and providing a type of a visual overview of coding patterns, by displaying co–occurrence of codes. They can also have a role in supporting activities such as checking coding reliability across documents or time or coders.

Step 1: Select the document you wish to report on in the Document Explorer.

Step 2: Click on the Make Report button. N4 opens up the Make Report dialogue box.

We will retrieve for this document its header, text and cross references.

Step 3: Click on the options you wish to retrieve, then click OK.

N4 opens up the report display of the text with codes listed below each text unit they reference.

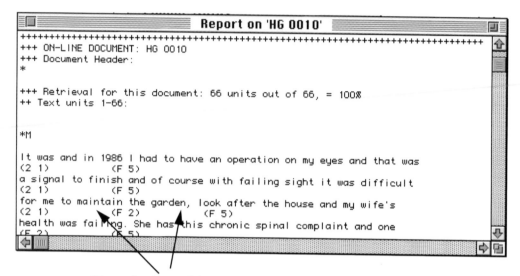

The coding is very light in this section. This section shows some degree of co-occurrence of codes (2 1) (F 2) and (F 5) in this segment of the text

14.3 Reporting a coding stripes

Finding ways to visualise the patterns of coding in a qualitative project is an ongoing challenge. A coding stripe provides a way to do this in N4. We will report a coding stripe for a document.

Step 1:   Select the document you wish to report on in the Document Explorer.

Step 2:   Click on the Make Report button.

Step 3: N4 opens up the Make Report dialogue box. In the section Coding to Display click on the radio button Coding Stripe, then click OK

The list of nodes that will be displayed as a Coding Stripe in the report

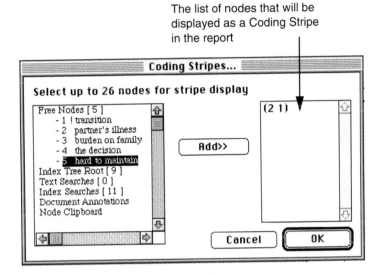

N4 opens up a dialogue box in which you are able to move, from one side of the display to the other, the nodes you wish reported as a Coding Stripe.

Step 4: Expand the index system on the left hand side of the display. Click on the title of the node you which to add to the coding stripe display. Click Add.

N4 shows the node (by its address) in the right hand side of the display. Repeat this process until you have moved all the nodes you want into the list.

Step 5: Click OK.

N4 opens up a document report showing coding by substituting alphabetic characters for node addresses and displays them in a series of columns parallel to the text. Our report shows only three codes, you may have up to 26 codes per report.

Coding key for the nodes used in
the coding stripe

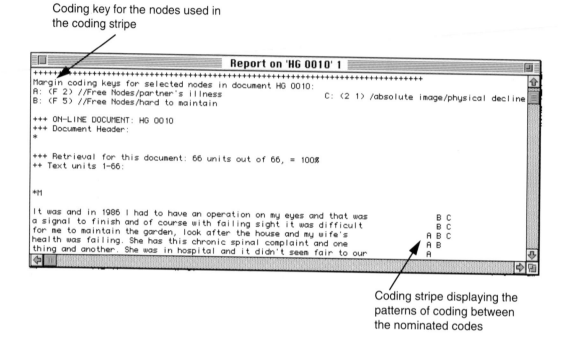

```
                                    Report on 'HG 0010' 1
+++++++++++++++++++++++++++++++++++++++++++++++++++++++++++++++++++++++++++++++++++++
Margin coding keys for selected nodes in document HG 0010:
A: (F 2) //Free Nodes/partner's illness
B: (F 5) //Free Nodes/hard to maintain            C: (2 1) /absolute image/physical decline

+++ ON-LINE DOCUMENT: HG 0010
+++ Document Header:
*

+++ Retrieval for this document: 66 units out of 66, = 100%
++ Text units 1-66:


*M

It was and in 1986 I had to have an operation on my eyes and that was      B C
a signal to finish and of course with failing sight it was difficult       B C
for me to maintain the garden, look after the house and my wife's        A B C
health was failing. She has this chronic spinal complaint and one        A B
thing and another. She was in hospital and it didn't seem fair to our    A
```

Coding stripe displaying the
patterns of coding between
the nominated codes

14.4 Displaying tables

N4 has the ability to export data from a project as a table. This facility has many uses and provides you with the options to export, to screen or file, a table which displays your coding. This is especially useful for displaying the output of a matrix or vector search. The exported table can show you whether or not documents are coded in each cell and how many text units or documents are coded.

Step 1:   Go to the Project menu and choose Export, then choose Matrix/Vector data.

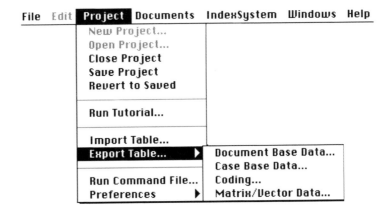

Step 2:   N4 opens a display from which you can choose what to display for each cell and where you want to output—to screen or to file. Make your choice, then click OK.

Cell display options: click on a radio button to select an option

Output can go to file or screen

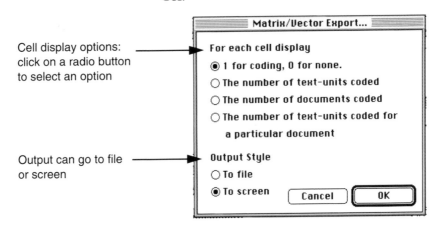

N4 exports the matrix as a table, with a "1" indicating coding and "0" indicating no coding for each cell. These types of tables provide a synthesised view of coding and are invaluable in finding ways to understand the results of your analysis processes.

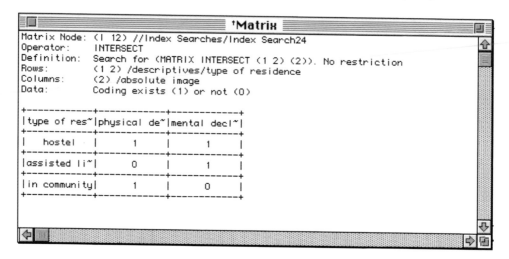

There are other facilities provided in N4 which facilitates the display of data for both presentation and interpretation. The *User's Guide* provides details of the other options such as exporting to specialized programs including *Inspiration, Decision Explorer* and *SPSS* or *SAS*.

The challenge for you is to utilise the tools in N4 to meet the needs of your processes. While we have covered the breadth of facilities in N4, there are many areas which we have not covered and those we have only just touched on. We hope that through the book you have become familiar with how N4 operates so that you are *better able to problem solve your way through learning* what you need for your project.

INDEX

INDEX